Penguin Specials
The Rise of Enoch Powell

Paul Foot was born in Haifa, Palestine, in 1937.
He was educated in Jamaica and later at Shrewsbury
and University College, Oxford, where he was Editor
of *Isis* and President of the Union. He spent three
years in Glasgow as a feature writer on the *Scottish
Daily Record* and has been an active trade unionist
in the National Union of Journalists. In 1967 he was
one of the Union's delegates to the Trades Union
Congress.

Paul Foot has worked for the *Sun* and the *Sunday
Telegraph* and for the past two and a half years has
worked on *Private Eye*. He is a member of the
International Socialism group, and is on the editorial
board of *Socialist Worker*. He is the author of
Immigration and Race in British Politics and
The Politics of Harold Wilson.

Paul Foot

The Rise of Enoch Powell

An Examination of Enoch Powell's Attitude
to Immigration and Race

Penguin Books

Penguin Books Ltd, Harmondsworth, Middlesex, England
Penguin Books Inc., 7110 Ambassador Road, Baltimore,
Md 21207, U.S.A.
Penguin Books Australia Ltd, Ringwood, Victoria, Australia

Published in paperback by Penguin Books
and in hardback by The Cornmarket Press 1969
Copyright © Paul Foot, 1969

Made and printed in Great Britain by
C. Nicholls & Company Ltd
Set in Linotype Times

Contents

256504

Introduction

This is not a biography of Enoch Powell. There is a good one of those out already (*Enoch Powell: The Man and his Thinking* by T. E. Utley, Kimber, 1968), and at least one more planned. Nor is it a fact-by-fact account of Powell's speeches on race and immigration. There is a good one of those out already too (*Enoch Powell and Immigration* by B. Smithies and P. Fiddick, Sphere, 1969). It is an attempt to trace the development of Enoch Powell's thinking and speeches on immigration and race – and, in doing so, to provide ammunition for a counter-attack.

The research for this book has consisted mainly of work among newspapers and newspaper cuttings, especially the *Wolverhampton Express and Star* and the *Wolverhampton Chronicle* which I have read for the relevant period. For the rest, I have had to rely on cuttings in libraries in several newspapers and at the Press Association (all these, I am sorry to report, are becoming increasingly difficult to consult). Such work among newspaper cuttings, however thorough, unfortunately cannot be completely exhaustive.

Anyone writing anything on race relations in Britain over the past fifteen years starts his research at the Institute of Race Relations. I have spent many happy hours in the Institute's library sorting through endless newspaper cuttings, and taking up the time of Mr A. 'Siva' Sivanundan, the librarian, and his jovial staff. I am grateful, too, to Nicholas Deakin, who has been working for the past five years on the Institute's Survey of Race Relations, and who wrote the bulk of *Colour and Citizenship* (Oxford University Press, 1969) – the massive result of that survey. He helped me with initial inquiries and read the manuscript.

During many visits to Wolverhampton, I spent much time in the library of the *Wolverhampton Express and Star,* and my thanks are due to the librarian there, Miss Iris Grainger.

Among those who helped me, either in interview, on the telephone or by letter were Mr Richard Reynolds, secretary of the Wolverhampton South West Labour Party; Mr George Thomas, former secretary of the town's branch of the British Immigration Control Association; Mr H. E. Lane, former leader of the council's majority Labour Group; Mr Peter Farmer, leader of the Conservative group; Mr Eric Robinson prospective Parliamentary Liberal candidate for Wolverhampton S.W.; Dr Garrett, Medical Officer of Health; who sent me back numbers of the borough's Health Report; Mrs Ruby Illsley, former chairman of the Health Committee; Dr J. F. Galloway, former Medical Officer of Health; Dr G. Lines, former Director of Education; Mr Eric Thorne, and Mr Tony Gardner, M.P., who were Labour candidates at Wolverhampton South West, respectively in 1959 and 1964.

Many of Mr Powell's colleagues past and present have been extremely helpful, notably Dame Patricia Hornsby Smith, Lord Boyd and Sir Edward Boyle.

Most importantly, if ironically, I am grateful to Enoch Powell. In February, a short report appeared in the *Evening Standard* 'Londoner's Diary' to the effect that I was embarking on this book. Immediately, I received a letter from Mr Powell offering all help with articles, speeches and information. As a result I had a long and fascinating interview with Mr Powell at his home, much of which is reproduced in the following pages. When I wrote to him in June asking for clarification on a number of points, he wrote back instantly, replying fully to them all.

The facts of Mr Powell's approach to race and immigration, as outlined in this book, show, I believe, a degree of inconsistency, uncertainty and opportunism which would put most politicians on their guard against the frankly hostile inquirer. Yet Powell seemed utterly confident of his consistency and correctness throughout. He has the ability not only of convincing others of his rectitude, but of genuinely and totally convincing himself.

His frankness was not, unhappily, shared by all his colleagues. A cautious letter to Sir Cyril Osborne, M.P., making a specific inquiry about an approach made by him to Powell in 1959; provoked a volley of good-natured abuse to the effect that 'it is monstrous of you so-called liberals to deny him (Powell) free speech'. The specific inquiry was not answered. More curtly, Mr Iain Macleod, M.P., replied to a long letter asking for help and information as follows:

'Dear Foot,
    Judging by your last book, I think I could indeed help you on the problems of immigration and race, but I am afraid I have no time to spare. Sincerely, Iain Macleod.'

Mr Harold Gurden, M.P., did not reply at all.

I have no thanks at all for Mr Ray Gunter, M.P., former Minister of Labour and of Power, who prevented me from obtaining a transcript of a profile of Enoch Powell on the BBC programme, Panorama. The profile was crucial in a great many ways, and the BBC promised to let me have it if I could obtain the permission of the participants. Powell's permission was, as the BBC agreed, implicit in his letter to me. Two other participants in the programme, Mr Nicholas Ridley, a Tory M.P., and Professor C. F. Evans, instantly replied to my publishers agreeing to the release of the transcript. The third, Mr Gunter, blankly refused, without giving reasons. The BBC were unable to edit out the Gunter sections, and the transcript was withheld.

Paul Foot, 7 July 1969

I was unhappy about what seemed to be the future of the British Empire. I could see that the only way I could do anything about the situation would be to enter politics. I was determined that I would do something to stop the disintegration of the Empire, which seemed imminent. (Enoch Powell, *Wolverhampton Chronicle*, 30 December 1955).

What I believe has been profoundly and generally resented is to be told at every stage that this or that action must be taken, not necessarily because we regard it as right or in the interests either of this country or of Rhodesia, but because, if we do not, 'it will mean the break-up of the Commonwealth'. Many people on being told this, say to their neighbours or under their breath: 'Let it break up then, so much the better.' (Enoch Powell, speech at Camborne, Cornwall, *The Times*, 15 January 1966).

Chapter 1
Grand Imperialist to Little Englander

In the spring of 1944, Field Marshall Auchinleck, Chief of the Armed Forces in India, set up the army in India Reorganization Committee under a lieutenant general, a brigadier, and senior representatives from all three services. Auchinleck insisted that the committee should also include an officer from army intelligence who was not a professional soldier. The Chief of Intelligence recommended a major on his staff, a very brilliant fellow, if a little odd, who was a professor of Greek. And so Major Enoch Powell was rapidly promoted to Brigadier, and ordered to Dehra Dun in the mountains where the Committee was based.

The main purpose of the Committee was to draw up a report on the necessary strength of the army in India after the war. The senior professional officers soon discovered that the young intelligence brigadier was a glutton for hard work. By the time they rose to set off on their early morning ride, Brigadier Powell had completed several hours work on the report. Taking time off only to complete his riding lessons (which, he discovered, Indian army officers could claim free), Powell devoted himself single-mindedly to the report. He was almost wholly responsible for the brilliantly argued chapter on officer recruitment after the war. The chapter dealt with the possibility of a large-scale invasion of India by Russia after the war, and suggested a strategy to counter it. The aim should be, suggested the report, to lead the Russians into India until they reached the area between the desert and the Himalayas. At that time, the Indian army would strike – but in order to strike effectively it required a large *force de frappe*.

How was such a force to be officered? Powell demonstrated that a large number of officers would be required; that India could only provide a certain percentage of men who had the educational qualifications; that of the Indians who had the necessary educational qualifications only a small percentage had the necessary 'officer qualities'. In conclusion, Powell wrote, India herself could provide only half the necessary officers for the next twenty years – during which time the other half, including its most senior officers, would have to be provided by the British. So lucid was the argument in Powell's chapter that his fellow-officers unanimously accepted it as part of the final report. It was not until Auchinleck himself saw the report that the Powell recommendations on officers were turned down. The argument, Auchinleck pointed out, was superb but the premises were formalistic if not nonsensical.

Powell's fellow-officers found him prickly, over-sensitive about his Midland middle-class background, which contrasted with their own simulated orthodoxy. He was at once hypnotized and irritated by the ease and arrogance of the officer class, and, while carefully studying every aspect of officer manners, he seldom missed a chance to demonstrate that he was 'different' – a cut below by birth, perhaps, but a cut above in every other way. When a colleague, in automatically polite small talk, remarked what a nuisance it was to have to work in the heat of a summer afternoon in Delhi, Powell replied that he greatly enjoyed working in Delhi during the afternoons, especially if he'd had a heavy lunch.

Of politics he talked little, though one of his colleagues remembers him saying that the war had been a great mistake on England's part. Few of his colleagues realized the political motivation behind his recommendations on the Indian army after the war – his deep and almost overpowering love for British imperial rule in India.

To this love, Powell has paid tribute on many occasions. Twenty-two years later he was still saying:

I fell head over heels in love with it (India). If I'd have gone there 100 years earlier, I'd have left my bones there. (*The Times*, 12 February 1968).

Powell had learnt Urdu ('to identify himself with the life and language of the country') and had grown deeply attached to the grandeur and patronage of the imperial way of life. He read Kipling voraciously, and even wrote poems in Kipling's style, praising the patterned discipline of the British Raj. Despite the precision of its logic, Powell's report to Field Marshall Auchinleck was probably governed not so much by the accuracy of the argument as by his burning concern that Britain should hold onto India and her army, if necessary forever.

In this view at that time, Powell was neither alone nor out of touch. To the vast majority of army officers and colonial servants in India at the end of the war, independence still seemed a faraway fantasy. The sting of the nationalist movement seemed to have been drawn by the war, which had, apparently, bound the immediate interests of British and Indians closer than ever before.

The speed with which the movement for independence gathered force after the war took nearly everyone by surprise. For Powell, independence was a horror to be avoided at all costs. He decided not to return to Sydney where, before the war, he had been a professor of Greek.

Instead, he travelled to England and rang Conservative Central Office. 'I had,' he told an interviewer later, 'always been an imperialist and a Tory.' (*Wolverhampton Express and Star,* 27 January 1950). A stern Black Country, middle-class upbringing had ensured that. The one way, he was sure, in which India could be saved from the ravages of socialism and independence was to convince the Conservative Party of the importance of maintaining the Raj.

The Conservative Party welcomed the young intelligence brigadier with open arms. They had few enough men of quality at the time to staff their party organization, and Powell was stretched to the limits on research work in a number of departments. To his horror he discovered that the Party had given up India for lost. Foreign and imperial affairs no longer dominated Tory Party thinking. Instead, the Party was desperately trying to construct new policies on such matters as housing and education. Powell applied himself rigorously to these, and became a keen and fashionable advocate of 'Conservative planning'. On India, however, he refused to be influenced by the shift in Party opinion. In January 1947, he was adopted as Conservative candidate at a by-election in the Yorkshire mining constituency of Normanton, which, in spite of a Labour majority of some 22,000 and one of the worst winters in British history, Powell fought with customary enthusiasm. 'Conservative planning' was the slogan he presented to the surprised Tories of Normanton, but on the subject of India he spoke in language to which they were more accustomed:

'The proceedings of the past few months,' he told his adoption meeting in the Baths Hall, Normanton,

have been characterized by a desire to get out of troublesome difficulties at whatever sacrifice of future safety. It would be a happy thing if our difficulties in Egypt and if the results of indecision in Palestine were the worst. They are not. We are incurring elsewhere ... graver dangers, notably in Burma and India. Such is the result of socialism in action in imperial affairs that it has threatened the eclipse of the whole Empire, which is the structure on which we are dependent for our very existence. If there is a way for the Empire to survive, and if that great chain of British territories round the world is to remain united, it can only be because through Britain is liberty and independence preserved. If that is not true, then we will perish in proving it otherwise. (*Pontefract and Castleford Express*, 31 January 1947).

Almost as soon as he returned from Normanton, where he collected 4,258 votes, Powell became involved in briefing his Party on a matter which aroused his deepest imperialist passions: the British Nationality Bill.[1]

Following a Commonwealth Prime Ministers' Conference in 1946, and the subsequent delegation of decision-making to a high-powered meeting of civil servants, the Labour Government sought to rationalize the existing law of imperial citizenship to bring it into line with the increasing independence of the old Dominions like Canada and Australia and the granting of independence to former colonies like India. In particular, the Canadian Citizenship Act of 1946, in which the Canadian Government had created a separate and distinct citizenship for Canada, meant that the old structure of British 'subjecthood' throughout the Empire had to be revised.

The senior civil servants accordingly advised that inde-

1. For the section on the British Nationality Act, I am wholly indebted to 'The British Nationality Act of 1948: A brief study in the political mythology of Race Relations' by Nicholas Deakin, published in *Race*, the quarterly journal of the Institute of Race Relations, July 1969.

pendent countries of the Commonwealth should be free to define their own laws of citizenship within a general framework of 'Commonwealth citizens', while the inhabitants of existing colonies should be classified as 'citizens of the United Kingdom and colonies'. These last should owe allegiance to the Crown and be subject to British dominion. Commonwealth citizens should be subject to their own laws while retaining membership of 'one great family of nations', with the Monarch as its symbolic head. The blanket classification of all citizens of Dominions and colonies as 'British subjects' should disappear.

These recommendations were accepted by the Labour Government and enshrined in the British Nationality Bill. The Bill was instantly attacked by the Conservatives. In the House of Lords, where the Bill first appeared, the Conservative Opposition forced through two amendments which effectively destroyed the Bill and lumped all Commonwealth and colonial citizens under the general heading of 'British subjects'. Thus amended, the Bill came to the Labour-controlled House of Commons, where the amendments were removed in the Committee Stage, and where, accordingly, the Conservatives voted against the Bill's Third Reading.

In the arguments against Commonwealth immigration in recent years, prominent Conservatives, especially in the Midlands, have argued that the 'traditional right' of everyone living in a country which formerly was part of the British Empire to enter Britain free of immigration control was the result of the British Nationality Act.

The former Conservative M.P. for Smethwick, Mr Peter Griffiths, wrote in his local paper:

Immigrants come here from the Commonwealth under the provisions of the British Nationality Act. This Act was passed by a Labour Government. (*Smethwick Telephone*, 20 September 1963).

And Mr Powell himself, in an interview in *The Times*, is reported to have argued that

the subsequent mass movement in immigration would not have occurred ... if the old concept of British citizenship had remained unchanged. (*The Times*, 20 December 1968, quoted in Deakin op. cit.)

15

In his introduction to the section in Immigration in his book, *Freedom and Reality,* (Batsford, 1969, p. 213), Powell wrote of the 'Commonwealth illusion':

The legal form which had been given to that illusion in 1948 by the British Nationality Act permitted the arrival of a big immigrant population...

In fact, the 'right of free entry' was not introduced by the Act, but merely rationalized by it. Moreover, the Conservative opposition to the Act was based at least to some extent, if not primarily, on the fear that the traditional right of free entry to Britain from all parts of the Empire and Commonwealth might now be threatened by the proposed division between 'Commonwealth citizens' and 'citizens of the United Kingdom and colonies'. Again and again, in the Lords and Commons, Tory spokesmen complained that the 'traditional hospitality of the Mother Country' was being begrudged by a mean, insular, socialist Government. The Tories argued that 'subjecthood' implied responsibility on the part of the Mother Country. If all the imperial peoples were 'subjects', then the masters owed them certain rights, chief among which was the open door to the Mother Country. To call them citizens, argued the Conservatives, might deny them that right.

Thus Sir David Maxwell Fyfe, later Lord Kilmuir, then Shadow Home Secretary, emphasized throughout his speech on the Bill's Second Reading, that the privileges of former 'British subjects' were imperilled by the Bill.

We have had much to offer the People of the Dominions and more to people of the racially distinct and smaller countries of the Commonwealth because ... we were proud in this country that we imposed no colour bar restrictions, making it difficult for them when they came here ... these people found themselves as privileged in the United Kingdom as local citizens...

There would be no point in passing such a measure unless the new category of the Right Honourable Gentleman – 'citizens' – were to have privileges and duties more extensive than the other classes of British subjects – that is, unless the old idea of common status, *and our proud boast of the open door in this country to people from all the colonies were to be destroyed.*

16

What I am asking for is the maintenance of the old basis of subject-hood, based on allegiance...

The next reason why we object to 'citizenship' is ... that we deprecate any tendency to differentiate between different types of British subjects in the United Kingdom. We feel that when they come to the United Kingdom there ought to be an open door and reception for every type. If we create a distinctive citizenship for Britain and the colonies, inevitably such differentiation will creep in. *We must maintain our great metropolitan tradition of hospitality to everyone, from every part of the Empire*. (My italics).

Lord Hinchinbrooke, one of the Highest Tories in the House of Commons, argued passionately against any threat or suggestion of closing the open door. 'Tamils, or natives of South Africa, he argued,

might come to this country at some stage and find themselves at a disadvantage as regards right of entry to the United Kingdom compared with those who are now resident in the colonies.

The Tories, in fact, had they been in power, would have upheld the principle of free entry even more powerfully than did the Labour Party. The Labour Home Secretary, Chuter Ede, assured the Tories that the last thing in his mind was to close the open door. Entry, he made it clear, would still be entirely free to all people living in all the Commonwealth. The Tories did not believe him, and based much of their case against the British Nationality Act on the grounds that it left the open door ajar.

No one was more responsible for the details of the Conservative opposition to the British Nationality Act than Enoch Powell. 'I remember,' he told me, 'briefing the Party on it.' Powell's recollection of that briefing was that, like his briefing to Oliver Stanley the previous year against conscription, it was ignored. His memory of the debates on the British Nationality Act is that the Act was not opposed powerfully enough by the Conservatives, but about his own opposition there is no doubt at all. In a speech to the House of Commons in 1953, Powell referred to 'those of us who inveighed against the British Nationality Act', and went on.

The British Nationality Act, 1948, removed the status of 'subject' of the King as the basis of British Nationality, and substituted for allegiance to the Crown the concept of a number of separate citizenships combined together by statute. The British Nationality Act thus brought about an immense constitutional revolution, an entire alteration of the basis of our subjecthood and nationality, and since the fact of allegiance to the Crown was the uniting element of the whole Empire and Commonwealth, it brought about a corresponding revolution in the nature of the unity of Her Majesty's Dominions. (House of Commons, 3 March 1953).

Powell, in short, was against the British Nationality Act because it dispensed with subjecthood, because it recognized the independence of the Dominions and many of the newer Commonwealth countries as a fact which could not be gainsaid by legal symbols like subjecthood and allegiance to the Crown; because, therefore, it gave the right to these new countries to break away altogether from the Crown and institute republics. Powell was against the Act because it wrote into British citizenship law the disintegration of the Empire. His opposition had nothing to do with the fact that it re-established the open door for all citizens of the Empire. On the contrary, one of his objections to the Act must have been, in Maxwell Fyfe's words, that it threatened 'our great metropolitan tradition of free entry from every part of Empire'.

The similarity between the views of Powell and his Party's spokesman, Maxwell Fyfe, on the issue was well illustrated by the 'personal allegiance theory' of imperialism, so well expressed in the following excerpt from Sir David Maxwell Fyfe's speech on the British Nationality Act:

I put this fundamental point to the Right Honourable Gentlemen and I make no apology for its stark and naked character; to a great number of the people of our colonies, especially our African colonies, the allegiance is not to a political system; it is to the King in person. Many colonial troops who fought in the war, fought for the King. That is not imagination on my part. I have consulted people at all levels, from ex-colonial secretaries and governors to those at a lower level who have been in personal contact with colonial peoples. (House of Commons, 7 July 1948).

Despite these somewhat selective sources, the 'personal allegiance theory' was dealt a hammer-blow not only by the independence of India but also by that country's insistence in

18

1949 on breaking all but the most formal links with the British Crown by declaring herself a republic. This act, and the Conservative Party's grudging acceptance of it, galvanized Powell, despite his promotion inside the hierarchy to the joint directorship of the Party's Home Affairs Department, to open opposition. 'I disagree profoundly,' he told an interviewer in his new constituency of Wolverhampton South West, 'with the way imperial policy has been handled in India.' (*Express and Star*, 21 January 1950).

The official reason for Powell's anger about 'imperial policy in India' was that a date had been set for Indian independence before any agreement as to what should follow it. The truth more probably was that Powell was opposed outright to the decision to hand over power. He remembers,

one evening, I think in 1947, after separation of India had become a political fact, walking about the streets all night trying to digest it. One's whole world had been altered.

The story goes that on one occasion he went to brief the Conservative leader, Winston Churchill on Indian policy and tried with a flood of statistics and logic to impress Churchill with the case for holding India, and, if it was abandoned by the socialists, of reconquering it. The argument must have been similar to that used in his report to Auchinleck several years earlier. According to his biographer, T. E. Utley,

Churchill rang up the research department to ask, 'Who was that young madman who has been telling me how many divisions I will need to reconquer India?' (*Enoch Powell* by T. E. Utley, William Kimber, 1968, p. 60).

Churchill's irritation over this interview could explain why Powell was never promoted to a Government post during the first four years of post-war Tory rule, when many of his contemporaries – Macleod, Heath, Maudling, for instance – were all taken into the Government.

Resentment against the abandonment of the most glittering jewel of Empire died hard in Enoch Powell, and in the 1950 election, in which he was elected for Wolverhampton South West, he raised the issue stridently. A local interviewer wrote of him:

Almost a blinding revelation was the realization of what a tremendous force for good the British Empire might become. He wanted to see the Empire growing and extending its influence for good. That is his ideal. (*Express and Star*, 5 January 1949).

Such ideals were speedily expressed in the House of Commons. A month after he entered Parliament, Powell spoke in a defence debate. This was no mealy-mouthed, 'non-controversial' maiden speech but a forthright appeal for rebuilding colonial armies to man the frontiers of Empire.
'We have lost,' he said,

the greatest non-European army which the world has ever seen, an Army which made possible, as did no other institution in the world, the active and affectionate cooperation of European and non-European...
If we are an Empire defending the Empire, we must draw far more than we do on the vast reserves of colonial manpower which exist within our Empire. The virtues which enabled British officers and British administrators to create this great army are not dead. The virtues which made the Indian army so great an instrument, although some of them are perhaps peculiar to the martial races of India, are paralleled in other parts of the world. Not only is it not impossible. It is imperative that we should create from the other parts of His Majesty's Dominions a replacement for that which we have lost.
One is shocked to see that in the last twelve months there has been a decrease of 15,000 in colonial manpower ... surely we are moving in the wrong direction .... That is the first direction in which we ought to look – the replacement of the Indian army. The demand that we shall do so rests ultimately on the conception that what we are defending, His Majesty's Dominions as a whole throughout the world, are in reality a whole.... We require ... a real recognition of a truly joint responsibility amongst all His Majesty's Governments for the defence of His Majesty's Dominions. I am well aware that such a demand raises far-reaching implications. I am not afraid of these implications, indeed I desire them for I am certain that unless we summon to the defence of the world-wide Empire all its resources, be they European or non-European, we shall fall under the load we are attempting to bear. (*Hansard*, 16 March 1950).

During the next three years, all these prophecies were rapidly disproved, and as imperial concession followed nationalist demand, Powell was moved to further fits of fury. All his anger was unleashed in an extraordinary Commons speech in opposition to the Royal Titles Bill, 1953.

Sir David Maxwell Fyfe, by now Home Secretary, moved the Bill in a spirit very different from that which he had displayed while opposing the British Nationality Act, briefed by Powell, five years previously. In office, Fyfe abandoned the symbolism of Crown allegiance and imperial subjecthood with which Tories in opposition 'justified' their Empire. Now, with as good a grace as possible, he and his colleagues were obliged to accept the 'new image' of the Commonwealth. 'The existing title of the Queen,' he explained to the House,

did not reflect the existing constitutional position under which other members of the Commonwealth are full and equal partners with the United Kingdom in the great family of nations. (*Hansard*, 3 March 1953).

The Queen's title, he went on, could not be, as theretofore, something which was laid down in Westminster – but something on which each member of the Commonwealth had to decide for themselves. The Bill was opposed, frivolously and futilely, by Emrys Hughes, William Ross, and a band of Scottish Labour patriots on the grounds that it did not grant a separate Royal Title for Scotland. Mr Cahir Healey, Nationalist Member for Fermanagh and South Tyrone, joined in the fun. These antics were brought to a halt when a furious Enoch Powell rose from the Tory backbenches to join the opposition. The Bill, he said, did three main things, for all of which there was only one word – 'evil'. First, the Crown was made divisible. The formula 'one sovereign, one realm' was desecrated. Secondly, the word 'British' was removed from before the word 'Commonwealth'. 'Why is it,' Powell asked, 'that this teeming womb of Royal Kings wishes now to remain anonymous?' Thirdly, the expression 'Head of the Commonwealth' now given to the Queen was 'essentially a sham'.

Towards the end of his speech, Powell abandoned logic and expanded on the real reasons for his opposition to the Bill.

The underlying evil of all this is that we are doing it not for the sake of our friends, but for those who are not our friends. We are doing this for the sake of those to whom the very name 'Britain' and 'British' are repugnant. We are doing this for the sake of those who have deliberately cast off their allegiance to the common monarchy ...

This was too much, not only for the Labour front bench, who had welcomed the new Bill, but for many more liberal Tories, who were horrified at these antediluvian assaults on Indian independence. Mr Godfrey Nicholson leapt to his feet, interrupting:

I beg my hon. friend to measure his words and to recognize the deep affection and feeling that exist throughout India towards this country.

Mr Powell:

I am obliged to my honourable friend. I, who have had the honour and privilege of serving with the Indian army during the war, am not likely to be unmindful of it; but it was an army which owed allegiance, an enthusiastic allegiance which was the very principle of its existence and its binding force, to the Crown. That allegiance, for good or evil, has been cut off, with all that follows.

At the end of his speech, Enoch Powell identified himself with history.

We in this House ... are in ourselves, our individual capacities, quite unimportant. We have a meaning in this place only in so far as in our time and in our generation we represent great principles, great elements in our national life, great strands in our society and our national being.

Sometimes elements which are essential to the life, growth and existence of Britain seem for a time to be cast into shadow, and even destroyed. Yet in the past they have remained alive; they have survived; they have come to the surface again, and they have been the means of a great flowering which no one had suspected. It is because I believe that, in a sense, for a brief moment, I represent and speak for an indispensable element in the British constitution that I have spoken.

(Spoken, perhaps, but not voted. For when the Scotsmen and the Irishmen divided the House, against the Bill, Powell did not join them in the lobbies. He abstained.)

Fifteen years later, in an appearance on the David Frost programme, Powell recalled his speech on the Royal Titles Bill as 'the thing that I'm most glad I was in Parliament to do'. By that time, he had in speech after speech, article after article, coolly dispensed with 'the indispensable element in the British constitution' for which he had spoken in 1953. The concept of 'one sovereign, one realm', of an indivisible British Empire under Her Majesty had been consigned by Powell to the category of 'past dreams'. Yet, in a sense, the recollection and the pride were justified. For Powell's speech on the Royal Titles Bill represented the first public demonstration of his most consistent ability: to construct out of reactionary prejudice (in this case, a love of Empire) an empty pyramid of formalistic logic, and to identify the whole with a Higher Destiny.

His defence of the indivisibility of the Queen's Title was not the last of Enoch Powell's speeches in defence of the Old Imperialism. As the months of Tory Government wore on, and as Enoch Powell was still not summoned even to junior office, his fury against the reformism of his own Party grew unabated. In November 1953, he spoke in a debate on Foreign Affairs in violent defence of the maintenance of British forces in the Suez Canal Zone.

The removal of these forces at this stage would have almost illimitable repercussions. ... What would be the encouragement given to those elements who are hostile to the association with Britain if they saw the ease with which by working up a fictitious or partly fictitious campaign of terrorism and threats Britain could be eased out of a position where she has been historically seated for so long? ... Suez is a nodal point in our defences...

My view of American policy over the past decade has been that it has been steadily and relentlessly directed towards the weakening and destruction of the links which bind the British Empire together.

MR CYRIL OSBORNE: No.

MR POWELL: American imperialism is advancing in this area from which they are hoping to eliminate us. They are eliminating us from a base which we have maintained with the blood of imperial troops in two world wars.

Throughout this speech Labour M.P.s interrupted Powell to ask whether he regarded the wishes of the Egyptian people as relevant to the maintenance of British troops in their country. Powell replied, in effect, that this was irrelevant. 'I do not believe,' he argued,

that the security of the Middle East or the Suez Canal will be safeguarded or can be safeguarded by any agreement which does not preserve in that area of the world an element of British combatant force. (House of Commons, 5 November 1953).

The interruption from Mr Cyril Osborne was symbolic. Osborne and a growing group of backbench Tory M.P.s were rapidly abandoning past notions of imperial grandeur and were tending to the view that the aims of American imperialism, far from threatening the future of Britain, were closely linked with the aims of British imperialism. Already in the Tory ranks could be detected the first faint stirrings of 'little Europeanism' – the abandonment of Empire and the military concentration of the metropolitan powers upon industrial units. To these men, Powell's ranting about the Grand Old World was embarrassing if not shocking. What they wanted was more 'realistic' conservatism – a relevantly narrow, mean, chauvinist conservatism to replace the Outward Bound savagery of former years. On 29 July 1954, twenty-eight Conservative M.P.s forced the Commons to a division through their opposition to their own Government's agreement with Egypt on the Suez Canal base. Among them was Enoch Powell. Mr Cyril Osborne, however, did not join them. That very month, he was starting his long campaign for the control of Commonwealth immigration, upon which subject Enoch Powell was to make no published statement for ten years.

At the annual meeting of Wolverhampton South West Conservatives on 20 November 1953, Powell delivered a further onslaught on his own Government for their proposed 'retreat from Suez'.

Whatever their popularity and whatever their past record a Government which was guilty of allowing Britain to be eliminated from the isthmus of Suez, in the conditions which exist there and in the Middle East today, would be judged at the bar of history and condemned. (*Express and Star*, 21 November 1953).

Powell himself regards this opposition to the Suez Canal withdrawal as his last fling as an Old Imperialist. 'I was,' he told me,

very active in organizing against the Suez treaty, and voted with the twenty-six and two tellers against it in July of 1954. But when we lost, I took the view that if we couldn't sustain our position in Suez, it was no good keeping the drums beating somewhere else. Our attitude over Suez had been that Suez was the last position we had to hold if our position in the Middle East was to be sustained. As Napoleon put it, 'war is a business of positioning'.

Now I remember very distinctly when the Suez group reassembled in November 1954, I went to the meeting just to tell them 'our work is done'. Our attitude had been that Suez was a key position; its strategical significance was such that a withdrawal from there was a sign that we could no longer maintain an imperial presence. I told them that if they were going to go on as we had done over Suez over other places in the area like Cyprus and Malta, I could not join with them.

This cannot be quite right, for in October of 1954 Powell told a meeting of his constituents that he 'accepted loyally' the consequences of the Egyptian agreement. 'For good or ill,' he said,

the Egypt question belongs to the past, but the Cyprus question is entirely different, because Cyprus is British soil and the Cypriots are British subjects. (*Wolverhampton Express and Star*, 23 October 1954).

The rhetoric of the old imperialism still came naturally to him and, in his constituency at any rate, he was still prepared to do what he was warning his Parliamentary colleagues in the Suez group not to do: to 'go on as we had done over Suez over other places in the area like Cyprus'. But in the more cloistered surroundings of the Conservative summer school at Nuffield College, Oxford, that summer, Powell had lectured on the Empire of England and was clearly beginning to change his mind.

The theory of the lecture ran as follows. True imperialism, the control of one nation over another, is only possible as long as the power in the dominant nation is not representative. As soon as Parliaments or representative institutions begin to replace institutions of arbitrary authority like the Church or the King, then its Empire is doomed. Representative government in the conquering country cannot for long maintain control over a country on an unrepresentative basis. The conflict between a democratic Parliament in the dominant country and its arbitrary control over another nation is bound to widen and become intolerable. Therefore, Powell seeks to argue, from the time of Cromwell any real hope of Britain maintaining an Empire was doomed. For Cromwell instituted a Parliament, sovereign over the King, and a British Parliament in undemocratic control of colonial nations would involve itself in a logical impasse which it could not survive.

Like so many Powellite arguments, the logic and language are so extravagantly precise that its flaws are, in the immediacy of reading it, not apparent. The major inconsistency, however, is that the heyday of imperialism was the heyday of British Parliamentarianism.

When Powell's thesis came up against such obstacles, it wandered off into Disraelian fantasies:

> There are millions who are bound to us by our military sway, and they bow to that sway because they know they are indebted to it for order and justice.

Powell concludes, perhaps more realistically, that it was the weakening of this 'military sway' rather than the logical inconsistencies in the imperial role of representative governments which hastened the dissolution of the British Empire: 'In 1941,' he wrote,

> it was proved once and for all that Britain could no longer protect her own. Though we won the war with Germany, we lost the war with Japan; and it is never healthy for empires to be defeated. It was henceforward clear that the realization of self-government in the dependent territories would end, as it had done in the self-governing colonies, in complete political separation. ('Tradition and Change', Conservative Political Centre, 1954, pp. 41–53).

The man who had walked the streets of London 'to digest' the independence of India, who had worked desperately for several years to retain imperial connexions in the sub-continent, and to champion, regardless of the will of the people there, the maintenance of British troops in the Suez Canal was beginning to construct a case to explain and justify in Conservative eyes what he was beginning to regard as inevitable: the End of Empire.

The following year, in another Oxford lecture, Powell expanded on his theme, urging his audience not to assume that

Parliamentary institutions were necessarily applicable to former colonies, but that they were

the only means practically available to us for accomplishing a transition which our own internal and external circumstances render unavoidable. For what follows after that transition . . . we cannot be responsible. Our true responsibility is that of achieving the transition itself with the least avoidable loss of honour and interest. ('World Perspective', Conservative Political Centre, 1955, p. 41).

This chain of thought was interrupted in December 1955 when the new Prime Minister, Anthony Eden, brought Powell into the Government as Parliamentary Under-Secretary at the Ministry of Housing.

The bulk of Powell's work at the Housing Ministry was devoted to the 1956 Rent Bill which made good the Conservatives' promise to set the landlord free. Rent control, and the security it offered to tenants, has been described by Powell as 'the ultimate evil'. He set himself rigorously to the task of removing it from a large section of privately-owned houses.

Immersed in the administrative work associated with the Rent Bill, Powell had little time to develop his conversion from imperialism. He rejoiced in the Conservative adventure at Suez in November 1956, personally regretting that British troops had not pushed through to Khartoum, but, as his Party emerged from Suez under the leadership of Harold Macmillan determined never again to make such a mistake for the sake of imperial sentiment, Powell was among the first to toe the line. By the winter of 1957, when he resigned from his post as Financial Secretary to the Treasury, over the Government's refusal to accept Thorneycroft's proposal for savage deflation ('It was,' he tells me, 'Thorneycroft's resignation, not mine') he was clearly converted to the 'wind of change'. The two major speeches he made in Parliament between resigning his junior Ministry and the 1959 General Election dealt with colonial affairs. Both are unrecognizable from the high-flown imperialism of Powell's Suez Canal speech in 1953.

First, Cyprus. In 1954, Enoch Powell had made it clear to his constituents that he was going to fight a 'sell-out' on Cyprus with the same ferocity with which he had fought the 'sell-out' in the Suez Canal. 'The Cyprus question,' he had warned, 'is entirely different because Cyprus is British soil and the Cypriots are British subjects.'

In his speech to the Commons on Cyprus on 19 March 1959, Powell welcomed the 'Macmillan plan' for independence. Quietly, he accepted that 'the physical, moral or sentimental reality of sovereignty has gradually fallen away'. Four years earlier he had argued for a British military presence at Suez, regardless of the wishes of the inhabitants. In 1959, he was telling the House of Commons that 'the utility of those areas (the military enclaves in Cyprus) to Britain will and must depend upon the good will of the people on that island'. In 1959, the converted Enoch Powell had a good word to say for Cypriot nationalism and a lot more about the 'responsibility of Britain to do no more than protect minorities, peace, justice and well-being'. Similarly, his speech on Hola Camp in July, in which he sharply attacked the refusal of the Colonial Secretary to hold two Kenyan Ministers responsible for the slaughter of eleven Mau Mau detainees, was entirely different in tone and emphasis from his imperialist ravings in the early 1950s. Harold Macmillan, who led his Party out of Suez holding high the banner of British imperialist prestige, but moving in the opposite direction – must have been proud of the most articulate and promising convert of them all, J. Enoch Powell.

Even out of the Government, however, Powell gave little of his time to the development of his thinking on imperialism. He worked feverishly on a long, loving history of the House of Lords. In July 1960, nearly a year after the Tory triumph at the 1959 election, Macmillan finally succeeded in wooing Powell back into his Government, and, later, into his Cabinet, as Minister of Health. During his three years in that office, the problems of colonialism did not unduly disturb him. It was after the resignation of Harold Macmillan and the elevation of Lord Home to the premiership that Powell, resigning from the Cabinet, applied himself to the problems of Commonwealth and Empire.

The argument about these matters in the Conservative Party in the years which straddled the 1959 election had been fierce, sometimes savage, but always one-sided. It consisted of a rearguard action by the old imperialists, championed by Lord Salisbury, against the granting of independence to former colonies on the basis of majority rule of the 'natives'. The argument centred upon Africa, and grew to a head with the granting of independence with a majority African franchise to Zambia in 1961. The old imperialists saw this as a betrayal of everything their fathers had taught them, and they argued in terms which were far too ideological either for the men who wanted to preserve their investments in Africa, or, more importantly, for the American Government and their intelligence arm in Africa. These last took the view from the beginning of the 1950s that a 'moderate' native Government was a great deal safer for investment and for cold war purposes than a white minority Government constantly fighting a war of oppression against the natives. With this view, the British Conservative Government and the bulk of their supporters consistently agreed.

Contemplating these arguments from the relative peace of the backbenches, Powell concluded that the majority were right. But he insisted, as is his wont, on drawing the ideological conclusions from the 'wind of change' and stating them in bold language which shocked conventional conservatism to its foundations.

His most emphatic statement was a series of articles in *The Times* of 1, 2 and 3 April 1964, which he wrote anonymously as 'A Conservative'.[1]

The second of these articles, entitled 'Patriotism Based on Reality, Not on Dreams', amounted to a stinging atack on the Commonwealth. The Commonwealth, he wrote, was 'a

1. There can now be little doubt that Powell wrote these articles. In a letter to me (30 June 1969) he writes: 'I have made a rule not to reply to any inquiries as to the authorship of anonymous or pseudonymous articles.' Asked about it at the time, he refused to confirm or deny that he was the author. A *Sunday Times* inquiry, using allegedly scientific methods to test the use of words and style, found that Powell was by a long way the most likely author. Apart from the style, the politics of the articles have been repeated since with such consistency by Powell (and by no other Conservative) that there can be no real doubt left. In his book, *Commonwealth for a Colour Blind World*, Mr D. Ingram identifies the author as Enoch Powell – and he is clearly right.

gigantic farce', a 'disastrous encumbrance from which Britain must break free ... Commonwealth preference has hag-ridden British commercial policy in the past two decades'. The monarchy was too sacred to be shared with people who did not want to share it, and in many cases despised it.

All this, argued Powell, demanded a new deployment of Britain's forces. Britain was not a Far Eastern power and her attempts to appear like one were ridiculous. Nor was Britain a Middle Eastern power. Cyprus, Aden, the Persian Gulf were all monuments to sentiment and history – not to reality. Conservative policy for the future should be directed to 'recasting our forces and defence policy on European lines' and to stop talking nonsense about 'brush fires' or Commonwealth trade.

The article caused a sensation, particularly in the Conservative Party, but the critical and supporting statements missed a significant passage dealing with a subject which had at that time almost been forgotten:

> To have our laws so far out of relation with realities was the cause of the massive coloured immigration in the last decade which has inflicted social and political damage that will take decades to obliterate.
>
> But it required a convulsion before the Conservative Party was forced to recognize, tardily, that a common citizenship of the Commonwealth was an outworn fiction. (*The Times*, 2 April 1964).

This was the first published statement in support of immigration control made by Enoch Powell, and even this was anonymous. The enormous majority of the Commonwealth immigrants now settled in this country entered in the years 1954–64. This was the period when, if Powell's later statements are to be believed, Britain was lighting her own 'funeral pyres' and inflicting on herself 'social and political damage which it will take decades to obliterate'. Yet in all that period, Enoch Powell made no public statement warning his countrymen of what he later told them was the disaster they were storing up for themselves. It was not until his anonymous *Times* articles in the spring of 1964 that we finally find Powell anonymously on the record against the open door.

The passage in *The Times* article quoted above, moreover, is a very different statement indeed to the imperialist phraseology of men like Powell who opposed the British Nationality Act of 1948. Powell's description of a 'common Commonwealth citizenship' as an 'outworn fiction' is the reverse of his and his Party's protests at the time of the British Nationality Act that common Commonwealth citizenship was a dangerous innovation. Powell and his colleagues, it must be remembered, fought the British Nationality Act not because they thought the Empire was finished, but for precisely opposite reasons – because they resented those aspects of the Act which dispensed with imperialist pretensions. They fought the law not because it was 'out of relation with realities', but because it weakened the Empire. The fought it, not because it opened the door to Commonwealth immigrants, but because they feared that the door might be shut. If Powell was right that the law 'was the cause of the massive coloured immigration in the last decade', his own and his Party's attitude to the law at the time when it was passed would have made that massive coloured immigration all the more inevitable.

Between 1948 and 1964, in short, Powell turned full circle on the issue of the open door for Commonwealth immigrants. The change corresponded at least to some extent with the development and change of his attitude towards imperialism. But in view of the importance which Powell himself ascribes to Commonwealth immigration in those ten years it is necessary, in the absence of any public statement, separately and in greater detail to try to trace Powell's approach to the problem during the period.

The first political demands for legislation to control Commonwealth immigration came in 1954 from Cyril Osborne and Norman Pannell on the Conservative backbenches. Their demands persisted, finding increasing favour with the Tory rank and file, throughout the 1950s. The answer they received from the Government was that control would be an admission that imperial traditions and 'rights' were no longer relevant – an admission that the Government were not prepared to make.

As Lord Colyton put it in the House of Lords:

We still take pride in the fact that a man can say *Civis Britannicus Sum* whatever his colour may be and we take pride in the fact that he wants and can come to the Mother Country.

31

As late as 10 October 1958, Mr Alan Lennox Boyd, later Lord Boyd, whom Enoch Powell described in his speech on Hola Camp as one of the greatest colonial secretaries in history could tell the Conservative Conference:

> To me it would be a tragedy to bring to an end the traditional right of unrestricted entry into the Mother Country of Her Majesty's subjects, and quite unthinkable to do so on grounds of colour. (*Manchester Guardian*, 10 October 1958).

And even in 1966, Lord Butler, the architect of the 1962 legislation, preferred to hark back to the sentiment, if not the reality, of the imperialist relationship:

> I think Britain, like Rome, should be *Civis Britannicus Sum* – I am a British citizen. I like to feel that the overseas people feel that they are British citizens. (*Listener*, 28 July 1966, p. 116, quoted in 'The Politics of the Commonwealth Immigrants Bill' by Nicholas Deakin, *Political Quarterly*, Jan–March 1968).

It was this sort of argument which moved the Conservative Cabinet, by a big majority, to take a firm decision in 1955 against Commonwealth immigration control – a decision that was reaffirmed in 1957 and 1958.

Powell now says that, as a junior Minister, he was opposed to this decision and in favour of control. He cites a meeting of the Home Affairs Committee of the Cabinet in 1956 which discussed the question and decided to support the Cabinet's line of no control. Powell insists that he was in the minority of the Committee, favouring control (I can find no evidence to support or contradict this). But if Powell was a supporter of control in Cabinet Committees in 1956, he was very shy about saying so outside them. On 31 August 1956, he spoke at a meeting of the Wolverhampton Branch of the Institute of Personnel Management. He was asked a question about immigration, and his answer is his only statement on the issue available on published record in any of the years before 1964:

> A fundamental change in the law is necessary before there can be any limit to West Indian immigration. It would be necessary to define a citizen of the British isles by his place of birth and his race. Such a

definition would put in the category of 'the rest' many British subjects, white, yellow and black, and would bring with it the necessity to discriminate against classes of citizens and to accord this or that class certain privileges. There might be circumstances in which such a change of the law might be the lesser of two evils. There would be very few people who would say the time had yet come when it was essential that so great a change should be made. (*Wolverhampton Express and Star*, September 1956).

Powell now explains that this statement was made out of loyalty to the Government line. He was, he says, a member of the Government, and was therefore forced to toe the line in his public utterances. His Wolverhampton statement needs to be looked at closely in that light. Its emphasis is entirely against control legislation. It talks of 'British subjects' and of the 'discrimination against classes of citizens' which a change in the citizenship law would entail, and argues that 'there would be a very few people who would say that the time had yet come when it was essential that so great a change could be made.' That is hardly the statement of a man who counted himself among those 'very few'.

In January 1957, Powell was promoted to the Financial Secretaryship of the Treasury, in which post he had even less to do with Commonwealth immigration than at the Ministry of Housing. An accurate and helpful picture of the discussions in the Conservative Government about immigration during 1957 is given by Miss Patricia Hornsby-Smith, then Parliamentary Under-Secretary at the Home Office, in a letter to me (22 April 1969):

My recollection of the immigration issue in 1957 is that the plain financial cost *vis-à-vis* the Treasury was of very little significance at that time, as we were in a period of high unemployment and the financial burden of immigration was not then an issue.
The Home Office was at pains to point out the increasing numbers arriving and the inevitable social consequences arising from demands on housing and education, together with the overburdening concentration in limited areas. At that time, we were in the throes of several constitutional moves to grant independence and the most vehement opponents who, on then perfectly justifiable political grounds, were the then Commonwealth and Colonial Ministers, felt that any such Bill would sour their negotiations with various African powers. In the case of

Kenya, it would have precipitated the anti-Asiatic moves now apparent...

At the Home Affairs meetings I attended, I think Henry Brooke was present rather than Enoch.

This view is substantiated by Powell himself who cannot remember the issue arising during his time at the Treasury. Yet the Treasury 'line' at that time, and at the time when the control legislation was introduced, was that immigration was beneficial to the British economy, and should not be slowed. The Treasury officials pointed out that the immigrant came into the country young, for the most part single and ready to work. The 'social costs' to the community of education and old age pensions were immeasurably less in the immigrant community than in the community at large, and that this was a once for all gain for the economy which would never be lost, however soon the immigrant workers were joined by their families.

But whatever the role of Enoch Powell on the immigration issue in the two years 1956 and 1957 in which he was in the Government, there can be no doubting his silence on the issue once he resigned from the Government in 1957. He then spent two and a half years out of government – in which time the flow of Commonwealth immigration into Britain, though slowed by the Thorneycroft deflation, continued without legislative control. In 1958, the Conservative Conference, against the advice of the leadership, passed a motion by a substantial majority calling for immigration control. In the summer of 1958, race riots broke out in Notting Hill and Nottingham. The subject of colour and immigration dominated The British Press for several weeks afterwards. In October and December 1958, Mr Cyril Osborne raised the issue in the Commons, demanding control. In all this period, through all this discussion and debate, Enoch Powell himself, according to all the published records, did not mention the subject once. Indeed, as he reveals himself, when an attempt was made to ecourage him into the campaign for immigration control, he turned it down.

This incident is best explained by Powell in the following extract from his interview with me:

POWELL: Sometime in 1958 or 1959 Cyril Osborne approached me. He said something had got to be done about immigration, and, knowing my views on the subject, he tried to get me to join him in his campaign – to raise it in Parliament and at the 1959 election. Given the situation I didn't believe it was easier to do it by Cyril Osborne's approach. I turned him down and Cyril felt, I think he felt, deserted by me.

Q. Why did you turn him down?

P. [laughs]. Well, I think recent events have proved why.

Q. What do you mean?

P. The more the harouche the more difficult it is to do it. It was a tactical problem. I thought that such a fundamental change in the law of the country was a monkey which was easier caught softly .... So I thought: I won't make a major speech about it. Someone's bound to ask me a question about it. A Conservative Government, if elected, will have to do something about it, to introduce legislation, and I didn't think it was a good idea to push it into the forefront at that time.

Q. But how can you say that? You've just been creating a fearful 'harouche' about it.

P. The situation now is very different. On so many issues one operates so differently in government, and a Conservative operates *very* differently – more so than a Labour man, perhaps.

If this was 'a monkey' which had to be caught softly, Mr Powell was calling so softly that nobody heard him. There is no record of any mention by Powell of the issue in the Commons, in his constituency or outside calling for control legislation to be introduced during the thirty months he spent out of the Government, and was therefore free to voice his own independent views on such matters. There is no record, for instance, of his giving even verbal support to the champions of control at the 1958 Party Conference, or in the 1958 House of Commons debates. As for the 1959 election, there is no record of anyone asking a question on the subject, as Powell had been 'sure' someone would. There is certainly no mention of it, not even a passing one, in Powell's election address. In a letter to me (24 April 1969) Mr Eric Thorne, Powell's Labour opponent at the 1959 election, writes:

Powell did not at any time mention immigration, though his supporters did (off the record, of course). Indeed we were all impressed by Powell's refusal to get involved in what was, even then, an explosive issue in Wolverhampton. You will no doubt recall that he took a lone stand over the Hola Camp controversy which we found (to be frank) disconcerting.

The *Wolverhampton Express and Star*, from the time the first black men showed their faces in the town, showed a keen (if patronizing) interest in the subject, and itself advocated immigration control from as early as 1956. Any news or comment on the immigration question (from both sides) always got wide coverage in the paper. Powell's off-the-cuff answer to a question at a meeting of the town's Institue of Personnel Management branch in August 1956 in which he prevaricated on the control issue, putting the argument against control, was fully reported under a large headline. It is difficult to believe, as Powell protests is the case, that the issue was raised regularly at Powell's meetings in 1959 – and almost impossible to believe that, if it was so raised, Powell advocated control legislation in his answers. The *Express and Star* is a daily paper, with a large reporting staff. In the 1959 campaign Powell held five meetings (rather more than his usual quota). In the first two, at Warstones and Bradmore, he declared:

The basic issue of the general election is simply whether the country wants a free economy or a planned economy.

In his eve of poll meeting, he spoke about the independence of former colonies, again demonstrating that his thinking had changed considerably since he advised Churchill to reconquer India. The 'right to independence,' he said,

is never in dispute. Until power is transferred, we are 100 per cent responsible. The tragic drama has arisen because our power and our responsibilities are unmatched. (*Express and Star*, 7 October 1959).

All these meetings were reported in the local paper's special election coverage. In none of these reports is the issue of immigration mentioned. If Enoch Powell, a resigned Minister and one of the most controversial figures in the Government Party, made a statement at any one of his meetings advocating control of Commonwealth immigration – which would have been contrary to Party policy – the *Wolverhampton Express and Star* missed a political story of some importance, and one which would have livened up what was, by general consent, a dull election.

After rejoining the Government in 1960, however, Powell became a firm advocate, again from inside, of control legislation. At a meeting of the Home Policy Sub-Committee under the chairmanship of Housing Minister, Henry Brooke, Powell remarked that the racial situation caused by immigration had gone 'beyond flashpoint'.

This meeting was one of many in the Conservative Government at that time in which Ministers wrestled with their consciences and backgrounds in an attempt to come to grips with 'the problem' of Commonwealth immigration. The objections to control were based in the main on the old illusions of imperialism. The Government's dithering on the question of Irish immigration, and the eventual exclusion of the Irish from the Commonwealth Immigrants Bill, published in November 1961, increased the unease with which Conservatives of the 'Radical Left' and the imperialist Right greeted the proposals. Even the *Daily Express* flirted fleetingly with opposition to control legislation (in an editorial on 16 November 1961). Formidable right-wingers like Mr Robin Turton, Mr John Biggs-Davidson, Sir Thomas Moore and Sir Douglas Glover made speeches against the Bill both inside and outside Parliament as did 'Tory radicals' like Humphry Berkeley and Lord Balniel. In the Cabinet, the merger of imperialists and radicals was strikingly illustrated by the two last-ditch opponents of the Bill: Mr Iain Macleod, fearful of its consequences in Kenya and Zambia where much of his work as Colonial Secretary was concentrated and Duncan Sandys, the Commonwealth Secretary, who was still worshipping at the imperialist idol of the 'open door'.

His colleagues in the government at that time recall that Enoch Powell shunned both of these extremes, and moved with the great swell of Tory feeling at the time: towards keeping out the blacks. Today, he talks of the 'terrible pressures' of the few months before the Bill, 'in which some weeks I used to get fifty to sixty letters a day on the subject'.

Yet there was nothing extreme or excessive about Powell's support for the Bill. He was still catching his monkey softly, and he did not make speeches in his constituency or outside praising the Bill or the Act after it became law.

As Minister of Health, he resisted demands from his more extreme anti-immigration backbenchers, notably Harold Gurden, M.P. for Selly Oak, Birmingham, to set up compulsory health checks at ports of entry, and, in January of 1962, as the Commonwealth Immigrants Bill was still struggling through the Commons, he turned down a demand to install temporary health checks at the ports during a smallpox scare, started by an outbreak among Pakistanis in Bradford.

His under-secretary, Miss Edith Pitt, acting presumably on her Minister's instructions, told the House of Commons:

In general, I have no reason to believe that immigrants from the Commonwealth have been responsible for bringing infectious disease into this country to an extent likely to involve a risk to public health. (Hansard, 11 December 1961).

Throughout his three-year period at the Ministry, Powell paid tribute to the work done in the Health Service by foreign doctors and nurses. In a debate on the emigration of doctors in 1962, for instance, he was interrupted by Patricia Hornsby-Smith:

'In order to get a fair analysis on the question,' she asked,

would my right honourable friend also give the figures of the Commonwealth and alien doctors who are working in the Health Service here?

MR POWELL: Not without notice, but ... they are undoubtedly an important element in the staffing of the hospital service. (House of Commons, 23 July 1962).

And the following year he did not stint his praise for

the large numbers of doctors from overseas who come to add to their experience in our hospitals, who provide a useful and substantial reinforcement of the staffing of our hospitals and who are an advertisement to the world of British medicine and British hospitals. (Hansard, 8 May 1963).

During Powell's régime at the Ministry of Health, Health Service recruitment drives for doctors and nurses in the West Indies and from India and Pakistan were not slowed down in any way. In the course of proving himself an efficient, if somewhat distant Minister, Mr Powell had no time to douse the 'funeral pyres' which he later complained, were piling up in those last years of Conservative Government while he was a Cabinet Minister. Nor did he have time to develop his views about imperialism and the Commonwealth. Only with the three *Times* articles did he spell out the logical consequences of his conversion, and openly declare against Commonwealth immigration.

By that time, opposition to uncontrolled Commonwealth immigration was more than respectable. By 1964, there was not a Tory M.P. to be found, and hardly a Labour or Liberal candidate either, who would speak out for the open door. Powell's declaration of support for immigration control in 1964 was an expression of mainstream opinion in his Party. Almost exactly four years after his articles in *The Times*, Powell said in a speech at Birmingham on the subject of immigration:

We must be mad, literally mad as a nation to be permitting the annual inflow of 50,000 dependants ... it is like watching a nation busily engaged in heaping up its own funeral pyre.

Yet in the years 1954–64 when the average entry of Commonwealth citizens was, approximately, 50,000 per year, if not more, there is not a hint in the speeches of Enoch Powell of all this funeral pyre-lighting. While Cyril Osborne battled in the face of unpopularity in his own Party and contempt outside it to control Commonwealth immigration, Powell remained silent. Even in 1964, his support for the 1961 Control Act was worded in mild language, incomparable in every way with the wild hysteria of his speeches four years later.

Powell cannot claim that his ten-year silence on the issue was because he had not come into contact with it. On the contrary, his positions in the Government, at the Ministry of Housing and Health, had placed him very close to the problems arising out of Commonwealth immigration, and his constituency was one of large-scale immigration throughout those years. Nor can he claim in his defence the doctrine of collective decisions, for in eighteen months in 1958 and 1959, during the race riots of 1958 and 1959 and full discussion of the issue in the Conservative Party, he publicly ignored the problem. The same goes for the twelve months following his refusal to serve in Sir Alec Douglas Home's administration. In government and out of it, in his constituency, in the Commons and in the country, Powell thought it right to make no public statement of any kind on the subject of immigration, even though begged to do so by his own colleagues.

Along with most of his Conservative colleagues, Powell's former commitment to Empire made him uneasy about the open attacks on immigration from the Commonwealth. His conversion from Grand Imperialism to a 'European strategy' was a long process, interrupted by spells of hard administrative work in government, and the relevance of immigration to that conversion was not spelled out until 1964. Like many Tory M.P.s Powell favoured the Control Act of 1962, but felt a little embarrassed by it in public. Unlike most contemporary politicians, however, Enoch Powell feels obliged to cope with ideological problems, and the shift in Conservative ideology from Imperialism to Europeanism was a matter which, for him, had to be worked out in ideological terms. This is the explanation for his *Times* articles and his subsequent speeches on the futility of Britain's maintaining former imperialist postures. As I write, and the comment and criticism of Powell fills the newspapers week after week, many commentators are giving him the credit for first having explained the Tory conversion from Empire to Little Englandism. That credit is richly deserved, but in granting it no one should fail to observe the most fundamental characteristic of the conversion – its cynicism.

For it is not hard to detect the reality behind the conversion. The British Empire was formed for one purpose only; the opening up of markets and the harnessing of raw materials and indigenous labour in foreign countries to the needs and priorities of British industry. This crude process required an ideology to sustain it in the pulpits, and this was found in the concept of common citizenship under the Crown. The Crown and her titles were very important, for they provided the necessary mystique for men like Disraeli to tell the Commons:

It is only by the amplification of titles that you can often touch and satisfy the imagination of nations; and that is an element which governments must not despise ... in announcing as Her Majesty will do that she accepts the title (Empress of India) confidence will be given to her Empire in that part of the world, and it will be spoken, in language that cannot be mistaken, that the Parliament of England have resolved to uphold the Empire of India.

All this touching and satisfying of the imagination of nations required something just a little more substantial than calling Queens 'Empresses', so the British borrowed from the Romans the concept of citizenship for their colonies.

The Romans had devised a system whereby those natives of their colonies who worked hard for the grandeur and privileges of the Roman aristocracy were rewarded with the 'prize' of citizenship. A Roman citizen then joined the ranks of the imperialists, and gained certain privileges. For instance, St Paul (of Tarsus), when he was flogged, made a violent protest, not against flogging in general which was all right for the natives, but against flogging *him,* since he was a Roman citizen.

The British were more generous. They made *everyone* in their colonies British citizens. It was an automatic reward for two centuries of being plundered. It cost nothing. And above all it gave the Grand Imperialists tangible proof that their system was justifiable before God, because all the people in the Empire, exploited alike, were simultaneously British subjects.

Parliament or no Parliament, the system worked tolerably well until after the Second World War. Then a combination of two major developments tore the flimsy ideology in pieces. First, there was full employment; the first time in world history when capitalist economies were able for long periods to expand without slump. With this development came the demand for labour throughout Western Europe, which could not be filled from European sources alone. West Germany and Switzerland, after soaking what they could from Southern Italy, sought immigrant labour from Greece and Turkey: France from Spain and Algeria. Britain, for two dangerous years, could not find the labour she required to fill the demand. Then, predictably, the labour began to come from the Commonwealth. The only conceivable practical advantage of the British citizenship with which the 'colonial peoples' had been fobbed off for 150 years – the right to travel without restriction to Britain, and to live and settle there as equals under the law – was being made use of.

Side by side with this development, came the revolution of the 'colonial peoples' against imperial power. Imperial power was shaken off, not, as Mr Powell would have it, because of the logical difficulties of reconciling Parliamentary government at home with arbitary government in the colonies, but because the 'colonial peoples' served notice on the invader to clear out. The two great bastions of imperialist ideology, loyal service to the Crown and a citizenship without privileges, were simultaneously threatened.

For the doctrine of 'equal citizenship' in the colonies had nothing to do with equality or with citizenship. It was a doctrine to be preached at Tory Party meetings, not a right to be taken up by the people who were fortunate enough to be given it. As long as black men worked loyally in the sugar and tea plantations, as long as they loaded the citrus and banana fruits for ninepence a day, as long as they turned out neatly on Sundays for church and every five years or so to cheer the relevant member of the Royal Family, they were equal. When, however, they appeared in the flesh in the street or town next door, not merely taking tickets on the buses or maintaining the dwindling profits of engineering firms or woollen mills, but taking, as of right, the services of health, education, even council housing, offered to constituents of decent white stock, their claim to equal citizenship was a shocking impertinence. Suddenly the florid rhetoric about the 'open door' turns into equally florid rhetoric about the desecration of 'England's green and pleasant land'.

In 1950, Powell's 'ultimate conception' was that 'His Majesty's Dominions throughout the world are in reality a whole', but by 1964, the 'natives' had taken control of the Dominions and the 'whole' had to be replaced by a narrow nationalism. Citizenship laws, Queen's Titles and all the other ideological cards in the game of British supremacy could be shuffled and discarded at will, and no one shuffled them more cynically than J. Enoch Powell.

Chapter 2
Immigration into Wolverhampton

In a book review given great prominence by the *Daily Telegraph* on 16 February 1967 and reprinted in his book, *Freedom and Reality,* Enoch Powell wrote:

> For over ten years, from about 1954 to 1966, Commonwealth immigration was the principal, and at times the only political issue in my constituency of Wolverhampton.

On 9 June 1969, he said, in a speech at Wolverhampton:

> At the General Election of 1966, I said that for Wolverhampton and other parts of the West Midlands, immigration and its consequences was and ought to be an issue, and had in fact been a pre-eminent issue there for a decade or more.

This was a theme which, since 1964, he has returned to again and again. The 'situation in Wolverhampton' has been given as the chief reason for his outbursts on immigration in 1968 and 1969. The uncertainty about the date when immigration became the 'principal and at times the only political problem in my constituency' is reflected in the columns of the local paper, the *Wolverhampton Express and Star,* which has always shown considerable interest in immigration and in race relations in the town. The first appearance in the paper of immigrants from the Commonwealth is in 1953, when one or two cases are reported of West Indians fighting cases at the Rent Tribunal. Throughout 1954, there is hardly any mention of 'the problem' at all, and in January 1955, the borough council politely refused a request from Smethwick Borough Council to a conference of local authorities in the area to discuss immigration. The Housing Manager summed up the view of council officials about the extent of the problem with the comment:

> There are not yet many people in the town's council houses. Those who are are look after their places well. There have been no complaints. (*Wolverhampton Express and Star*, 19 January 1955).

That same month, immigration had caused enough concern in Birmingham to persuade the Labour council to send a delegation to discuss with Home Office Junior Ministers, led by Sir Hugh Lucas Tooth, Parliamentary Under-Secretary, the case for immigration control (some time after this meeting, the Cabinet decided definitely against control). Alderman W. T. Bowen, leader of the Birmingham delegation, expressed 'extreme concern' at the pressure on services, especially housing, caused by the new immigration.

In Wolverhampton, there was no one to express such concern. The town clerk, Mr A. G. Dawtry, was quoted as saying:

Coloured people in Wolverhampton have not created sufficiently great problems for the council to have to consider such action themselves. The coloured population of Wolverhampton has shown itself to be very law-abiding. (*Express and Star*, 19 November 1955).

The managing director of a big rubber firm, employing fifty or sixty coloured workers, was quoted as saying:

There is no antipathy of any kind between white employees and the coloured men. (ibid).

At the 1955 election, none of the candidates identified the 'principal if not the only political problem' enough to raise it once. Mr Enoch Powell, for instance, had a great deal to say about the evils of rent restriction (21 May), price control (25), bureaucracy (19), but nothing at all about immigration. Small wonder that the *Wolverhampton Express and Star*'s exhaustive survey on the 'vital issues of this election' in Wolverhampton and the Black Country listed a large number of problems, but found no mention of immigration from any of its respondents.

Later in 1955, Alderman H. E. Lane, leader of the majority Labour group on the council, set up a council inquiry into the immigrant concentration in the Waterloo Road area, and Lane referred the whole matter to a full-scale inquiry.

The results of the inquiry were published in January 1956, and drew some comment from the local paper, which estimated that there were under 1,000 coloured people in Wolverhampton.

'One of the surprises of the report, it is understood,' concluded the *Express and Star* leading article,

is that worse overcrowding conditions exist in cases of Irish and continental immigrants. The coloured folks' accommodation is thought to be capable of favourable comparison with some English homes. (*Express and Star*, 12 January 1956).

The Labour council, just to make sure, set up a sub-committee, under Lane, to investigate the matter. Despite extensive publicity, the sub-committee clearly never got off the ground. When I interviewed Lane in March 1969, he could remember nothing at all about the committee, and strenuously denied that it had ever been set up. Both the town's J.P.s were asked to serve on the committee. The local Press reported an enthusiastic response from Mr John Baird, Labour M.P. for Wolverhampton North East, the area in which most of the town's immigrants lived. Baird promised support for the sub-committee, and promised also to contact Mr Powell, the town's other M.P., and seek his help. On 11 January, he 'had not yet had a chance to speak to Mr Powell, but would be contacting him soon'. There is no record of any such meeting. Powell does not remember it, and Baird is dead. Mr Baird's agent at the time, Mr Frank Mansell, told me curtly: 'I never had anything to do with any of that.' Whatever Powell's reaction to that approach, Baird devoted himself enthusiastically to promoting good race relations in Wolverhampton and to fighting against racial discrimination. By contrast, Powell played no part whatever in any of these activities.

The inquiry into Waterloo Road and the setting up of the sub-committee produced a number of letters to the local Press on the subject of immigration. In those first few months of 1956, the letters were almost all friendly:

'I should like to point out,' wrote G. Preston, a shopkeeper from Lanesfield,

that these people are very friendly and are most anxious to come into our way of living and our way of life. (14 January 1956).

And from Mr A. W. Styche, secretary of the Wednesbury branch of the right-wing British Iron and Steel and Kindred Trades Association:

I can say, as a factory worker working amongst them, that they are friendly enough. It has been stated previously that they do not possess the grit to do a hard day's work. Again, I beg to differ, because I see them hourly working alongside our own workers. (18 January 1956).

During the 1940s and 1950s, the town of Wolverhampton, traditionally based on small metal and engineering industry and the values of the small businessman, was going through an industrial revolution. Her small industries were rapidly being swallowed by large-scale firms, especially foundries and in one case, a big tyre factory. The ethos of 'the small man' lingered on, but the town was becoming as dependent on big firms as any other in the land. A statistical study of the town in 1961 found that 56·7 per cent of the town worked in manufacturing industry and only 5·7 per cent in 'professional' services.

This increasing concentration of industry was the main reason for the immigration into the town. As a feature writer in the *Express and Star* put it (19 January 1956):

If Britain's present boom is to be maintained, more workers must be found. Where? The new recruits to British industry must come, it would seem, from abroad, from the colonies, Eire and from the continent.

Some research into the effect of coloured immigration into the industry of the Midlands had already been done, notably at Fircroft College Birmingham, whose warden, Leslie Stephens, declared in March 1956:

Some engineering firms employing more than 25 per cent coloured workers are hoping that others will not find out that they are onto a good thing. At an engineering works employing more than 50 per cent coloured workers, the assistant works manager reported that they were keener than other workers on overtime, though they required more supervision. (*Birmingham Evening Post*, 21 March 1956).

In April, the *Express and Star* reported that

another 1,200 West Indians have arrived in this country. As with previous contingents, a proportion of these job-seekers are coming to the Midlands. They are, of course, British subjects and have a perfect right to come here and try to earn a living. Many are better behaved than some of their white cousins in this country and have proved themselves industrious workers. (9 April 1956).

By now, however, the industrial boom which had surprised even the most optimistic economists by lasting almost without pause from 1951, was on the wane. For the first time since the war, it looked as though the permanent expansion of the British economy would have to be slowed. Balance of payments problems and 'overheating' caused by a lack of investment and consumer boom, forced the Chancellor to start cautiously cutting back on public expenditure.

The recession which followed in the wake of the cuts gave rise to old fears among workers of unemployment and slump. The confidence of the early 1950s quickly evaporated. The first (very few) letters complaining about West Indians began to appear in the local Press. At a trades council meeting in June, a delegate from the Transport and General Workers' Union called for some action from the local authority to deal with the problems created by the existence of some 2,000 coloured people in the town. 'These people,' he said,

have come to stay and we must not bury our heads in the sand and say that they may go before long. They are raising families here, and we have got to make provision for them.

He was answered by Councillor Bagley (later to become Mayor) who said that the problem was being greatly exaggerated. There had been one case of TB among coloured people in the town, and there were no more than 100 Jamaican children in the town. 'Concern' was also expressed by the Wolverhampton Employment Committee and the Rotary Club. The *Express and Star* for the first time called for some measure of immigration control (in an editorial on 25 June 1956). Yet the sporadic complaints were justified neither by overwhelming public opinion nor by the social factors. In February 1957, Wolverhampton's Medical Officer of Health, Dr J. F. Galloway, went to the annual conference of the Royal Society of Health, where he referred in passing to West Indian immigration into Wolverhampton. Dr Galloway's articles and statements on the subject in the mid-1960s furnished the pretext for widespread campaigns against immigration. At the Royal Society Conference in 1957, he was contemptuous of exaggeration:

My authority is surprised and pleased how minor a problem the immigrants present. There is not a great deal of difference between a cross-section of coloured immigrants and some of our own people. They may keep their curtains drawn, but they are not a great deal different to other people. One begins to wonder whether it is not our own intense patriotism that makes us blind to our own deficiencies. Some immigrants are above the standard of our own people, and the sooner we stop all this 'blah' about 'the problem' the better. (*Express and Star*, 28 February 1957).

The Medical Officer of Health, then and now, probably knew more about these matters than most local officials and councillors, but the local authority as a body took no steps seriously to find out what sort of people were coming into Wolverhampton, what their problems were and how best they could be assisted. Crude statistics were compiled (like the number of black children in nursery schools) but it is a fair guess that no one on the local authority knew anything about where the immigrants came from and their background. Some assistance was given them by a survey conducted among the town's coloured people by the Wolverhampton Fabian Society in the summer of 1957. Fifty-six people were interviewed, as a representative cross-section of the coloured community. Only two were over forty. All of them – men and women – were working, mostly in factories. The majority of men gave their occupation in Jamaica as 'farmers' and the women as 'dressmakers', which meant simply that they had come from the rural areas of Jamaica, and that they had probably been unemployed there.

Late in 1956, the Wolverhampton Borough Council affiliated to the newly-formed Commonwealth Welfare Council, a body for voluntary provision of advice and assistance to immigrants in the Black Country. The councils affiliated to the council included Walsall, Wolverhampton, West Bromwich, Smethwick, and many of the smaller boroughs in the area. In 1957, a secretary was appointed – Mr Geoffrey Ayre, a Christian pacifist who had been a conscientous objector during the war and had given up a small business to work at the Clifton Institute in Birmingham. Ayre set up 'surgeries' in each of the affiliated towns, and spent the best part of the next ten years operating a one-man welfare service. He reckons that in that time he dealt with some 38,000 individual cases in six local authorities and that for many of his ten years in that area he knew of every coloured family in the area. The service he provided was almost wholly advisory. But in that time he got to know most local officials and councillors and the number of complaints with which, with a phone call to the relevant office, Ayre managed to deal are incalculable. He acted as an immigrants' Ombudsman, paid by the local authorities, with no power but with a great deal of influence. In hundreds of cases every year, he acted as a 'safety-valve' through which complaints could be directed, treated sympathetically and often solved.

Wolverhampton was the biggest town in Ayre's area and he spent every Tuesday in the town for ten years. The 'surgery' opened at 10.30 in the morning, but people would often start queuing up at about 7.00 a.m. He seldom got away at the appointed time of half-past five. There is no one in Britain who knows half as much about the process of immigration into Wolverhampton as Geoffrey Ayre.

Looking back on those early years, Ayre remembers two aspects of the immigration which distinguished the situation in Wolverhampton from elsewhere in the Black Country. The first was that the immigration at that time was almost exclusively from the rural areas of Jamaica. 'These people,' he told me were from the under-employed and backward countryside of Trelawney and Hanover. They would have been out of place in Kingston, much less in Wolverhampton. They were peasant people, many of them aggressive in their distaste for town life and town habits. And all this was accentuated by widespread illiteracy. Many would come to me with forms which they would ask me to read for them. There was a desperate need all the time for the simplest forms of assistance, but the local authority never did anything unless I pushed them. Wolverhampton was fortunate too in having some very good and sympathetic officials – a very good housing manager and education director, and an excellent Youth Employment Service. But even with these men around, there was very little done to assist the immigrants, in spite of the striking difference between their background and their new environment.

The second, perhaps related, aspect which Mr Ayre remembers is that the Wolverhampton immigration brought with it many more children than the immigration into other Black Country boroughs. In 1957, for instance, the number of women and children outnumbered the men, while in all the other Black Country boroughs (and certainly in London and Birmingham) the men greatly outnumbered the women and children until the large-scale 'beat-the-Act' immigration of 1960 and 1961. Ayre welcomed this. 'The very large increase,' he told the local Press,

of Commonwealth women and children coming to join their menfolk gives me comfort. The communities are developing a sense of greater security and permanence. (*Wolverhampton Chronicle*, 10 April 1959).

This has been the experience of race relations workers not only in Britain but in all other countries of large-scale immigration. Strife, resentment, aggressiveness, racial antagonisms, homosexuality and prostitution are more likely to arise out of immigration where the working men are not joined by their families and where the immigrant community is based not on family units but on workhouses or hostels. This is the most obvious instance where the crude generalization about immigration later stated by Enoch Powell – that 'numbers is of the essence' – is the reverse of the truth. Mr Ayre remembers that the fact that the larger immigration of women and children into Wolverhampton immigration was a strong counter to the less hopeful aspects of that immigration: its peasant origin.

Geoffrey Ayre came to Wolverhampton just in time. From the beginning of 1958, there are several examples of what might have happened had there been no 'safety valve'. In February 1958, a Jamaican family called Moody were denied a house in a housing estate outside Wolverhampton on grounds which were frankly racial. Public reaction to this colour bar was hostile. Several letters printed by the *Express and Star* were almost all 'disgusted' at the discrimination. Three months later, the Scala ballroom in Wolverhampton declared a bar on all coloured young men who came without partners. Again, this provoked a considerable distaste, notably from Mr John Baird, M.P., who attempted in court unsuccessfully to oppose the granting of a licence to the Scala ballroom.

Baird and a number of councillors publicly campaigned against the Scala colour bar, and Baird introduced a Bill in Parliament banning racial discrimination in public places. The local council referred back to its by-laws on the grounds that they ought to contain clauses banning colour bars.

The 1958 summer riots in Notting Hill and Nottingham prompted Baird, and another ardent opponent of racial discrimination, Councillor J. K. Woodward, to set up vigilante groups to tour the town at night to see that no racial trouble exploded. A teenage riot in Dudley directed against coloured people provoked a storm of criticism from the local paper:

> In Dudley, the black people were merely the innocent victims of an outbreak of lawlessness. They suffer from unemployment and bad housing ... add to these difficulties the experience of being chased along the streets of a strange city by a yelling crowd for no other reason than that they were black, and I marvel at their patience and good behaviour. (Editor, *Express and Star*, 5 September 1958).

By the 1959 election, therefore, the situation was as follows. Some 4,000 immigrants, mainly Jamaicans from rural backgrounds, had come to live and work in Wolverhampton. Their coming and their settling had been subject to no government planning or assistance, save the work of one Commonwealth Welfare Council Officer. The attitude of the local authority was well summarized by Alderman H. E. Lane, chairman of the Housing Committee, in reply to a demand for the council to set up a special housing association for coloured people: 'The attitude of the corporation,' declared Lane,

> has always been that it is wrong in principle to differentiate in any way whatsoever between citizens on grounds of colour. (*Express and Star*, 29 July 1959).

The immigration had been greeted with considerable resentment by substantial numbers of the population, though Mr Baird's suggestion at a socialist meeting in St Pancras that 'in areas like Wolverhampton, there is racial prejudice in as much as 40 per cent of the population', (*The Times*, 30 September 1958) was certainly an exaggeration. This resentment was kept very much below the surface and was of little or no political significance. Mr Baird suggested after the 1959 election that he had lost votes as a result of his stand against racialism, but the swing against him in Wolverhampton North East was no greater than the average swing against Labour throughout the country. Eric Thorne, the Labour candidate for Wolverhampton South West, who lived in Birmingham at the time, writes to me that

the beginnings of the current immigration problem were very much in evidence during my candidature (from 1956 onwards). They were issues in which we were on the defensive.

All the same, they were issue which were seldom raised and which few people thought right to raise. Moreover, there was a groundswell of opinion against racialism and against colour bars which was enough to make people think twice before stridently raising the issue in public.

The situation was accurately summed up by Geoffrey Ayre in his meeting with the Prime Minister of Jamaica, Mr Norman Manley, who was touring Britain in the aftermath of the Notting Hill and Nottingham riots.

'I told him,' wrote Ayre,

that, so far, there had been no disturbance in Wolverhampton, and he thought it unlikely that there would be because there was no trigger mechanism to cause a flare-up of racial prejudice. I told him that there had been no disturbance. . . . Over the past few months we have worked hard for racial integration in this area. Because of this, the resentments of the people have been channellized to us and it has provided an outlet. . . . Mr Manley said he was very glad about the position in Wolverhampton. (*Express and Star*, 19 September 1958).

The lack of a 'trigger mechanism' to set off a racial explosion existed throughout Wolverhampton society. The local authority, while inactive on the question of immigration, openly frowned on discrimination. So did the churches. So, vociferously, did the local Press. Mr John Baird and his supporters openly campaigned and demonstrated about it. But what of Mr Enoch Powell?

Mr Powell had been brought in contact with the immigration question on more than one occasion. In August 1956, as we saw in the last chapter, he had dealt with a demand for control at a public meeting by putting the case against it.

There is, unhappily, nothing else on published record, nor in any councillors' memories about Powell's response to Wolverhampton immigration in the 1950s. In the summer of 1958, the Press reported that the director of the Scala ballroom, who had ordered the colour bar, was to 'seek a meeting with Powell' on the question of the ban put on the ballroom (as a result of the colour bar) by the musicians' union. He got no support either from Mr Powell or from local Conservatives, and by February 1959 the ballroom had changed hands and was again open to all. In July 1958 Powell and Baird were invited to speak at the quarterly meeting of the working men's clubs and Institute in Wolverhampton Civic Hall. Baird spoke first and violently attacked the increasing incidence of colour bars in working men's clubs. Powell's speech, on the other hand, scrupulously avoided the issue and dealt in eloquent frivolity with 'the good administration of these clubs'. Powell was asked to attend the opening meeting of the Commonwealth Welfare Council, but did not go.

Geoffrey Ayre says he has never met Powell, and cannot remember a time when Powell took the slightest interest in race relations in Wolverhampton. When I asked Powell about Ayre, he clearly had no idea to whom I was referring and muttered vaguely about 'someone based in Birmingham ... a candidate'. Mr Reginald Eyre was an official of the Conservative Party in Birmingham, and later Member of Parliament for Birmingham, Hall Green. But of Mr Geoffrey Ayre, who spent ten years in Powell's constituency working with the coloured people there to create better race relations, Powell has no recollection. Certainly before 1959, and most probably after it, Powell took not the slightest interest in immigration into his constituency and the multiple problems arising out of it.

All this, in his disarming way, Mr Powell admits quite freely. 'From then (1956, onwards) he told me,

the crucial issue, dwarfing all others, was the changing of the citizenship laws. While that issue remained unsolved, it was quite useless in my view to find out the figures about leprosy and gonorrhoea, or to deal with the broader issues of community relations. All these were just palliatives compared with the urgent requirement of changing the citizenship law. The only answer I had to constituents' pleas and complaints was that we must change the citizenship laws so that the dimensions must stay as they are.

The implications of this statement need to be spelt out more clearly. Powell is saying that the problems created by immigration into Wolverhampton, problems of overcrowding in housing, problems of language and illiteracy, problems of racial discrimination, of cheap labour, of food and drink and entertainment – all these real, human problems in the area were 'dwarfed' by the need to change citizenship laws so that the problems could be kept in small dimensions. So much were they dwarfed by this enormous problem, moreover, that any application of any kind to these 'minor' problems was out of the question. Enoch Powell is saying openly that race relations in Wolverhampton were, as far as he was concerned, not worth bothering about until the citizenship laws were changed.

To illustrate how he put his theory into practice, Mr Powell told me an extraordinary story. He claims that,

some time late in 1958 or early 1959, I had a sharp passage of arms with Alan Lennox Boyd (now Lord Boyd, then Colonial Secretary). Alan wrote to me asking if I could do something about a West Indian who had been barred from a housing estate. (It was outside my constituency but I imagine Alan thought it was inside it.) I replied to him very sharply in terms that it was no good dealing with the details when the real issue, the citizenship laws, was not touched.

Lord Boyd cannot recall this incident, despite making some inquiries about it among his former staff at the colonial office.

The implications of Mr Powell's story are most interesting. The convenient argument for immigration control, both before and after the Act of 1962, was that control would improve race relations. The tighter the control, argued its supporters, the less the racialism. Powell took this argument one step further. He says he wrote to Lennox Boyd that there was no point in combating racialism unless control were introduced; that, without control, racial discrimination might as well be given a free run by Members of Parliament and leading members of the community; that it was little short of shocking that Ministers of the Crown should be mucking about with alleged cases of racial discrimination while the 'real issue' (immigration control) 'remained untouched'. The racial problem, therefore, boiled itself down to a single, simple demand: Keep Them Out.

The attitude of Geoffrey Ayre, who saw a great deal more of Wolverhampton than Enoch Powell and understood the problems of immigration into the town much better, was quite different. Ayre regarded immigration control as an irrelevancy. Control or no control, he argued, the demand for labour in Wolverhampton would not have changed and new workers would have come from somewhere. The crucial issue was the relationship between these new workers and the indigenous population which, given the shortages in the social services, particularly housing, could easily degenerate into friction, or even violence. The first open signs of such friction appeared in Wolverhampton in 1961.

On 18 July 1961, eight members of the newly-formed British Immigration Control Association travelled from Birmingham, where the Association had just been formed, to Wolverhampton. They distributed several thousand copies of leaflets drawing attention to the high rate of disease and unemployment among immigrants and calling for a complete ban on immigration. The leaflets advertised a BICA meeting that evening in the Wolverhampton Grammar School.

The handing out of leaflets for a few hours was the only form of advertisement for the meeting, yet the Grammar School that evening was packed. At least 300 people turned up to hear two officers of the Association, and a Birmingham councillor called Charles Collett who, since 1954, had been warning of the menace of coloured infiltration and a 'piebald population'. Ayre, who went to the meeting, thought it

the worst I have ever attended. It was one long catalogue of the crimes, disease and fecklessness of coloured people. None of it had anything to do with the facts.

The audience, however, received the speakers with acclamation, and about thirty of them came foward after the meeting to elect a committee. A building merchant called Joe Holland who had stood as a Conservative candidate for the council but was later to be elected as an independent, without Conservative opposition, became chairman. The secretary was Mr George Thomas, a welder who lived in a cul-de-sac called Paget Street, most of whose houses had come under immigrant occupation. The joint treasurers were Mr A. J. Bateman and Mr Birch, both machinists, and the rest of the committee consisted of three other skilled workers and two housewives, one of whom, Mrs Manning, resigned some months later.

The branch committee met regularly for more than a year after the founding meeting, but, especially after an application for a further meeting in the Grammar School had been turned down by the council's education committee, they made no real effort to hold other meetings or distribute propaganda. According to Thomas, the only committee member I was able to contact, most of the committee's work was taken up in dealing with complaints from individuals about immigrant transgressions. There was very little attempt, as at Smethwick, to introduce the issue into Wolverhampton politics.

Mr Thomas does remember, however, the occasion when the BICA branch committee visited Enoch Powell in the Conservative rooms to discuss with him the problems caused by immigration.

'He was,' remembers Thomas,

just the opposite to what he is now. He was all for the immigrants. We had a lot of examples of the dirty filthy habits of immigrants which we could prove, and we asked him to act on them – or at least make a fuss about them. He was very polite, very sociable, but he tried to sidestep all our complaints by suggesting we take them up with the relevant department of the local authority.

'We didn't get any satisfaction from him,' reflects Thomas.

I remember coming away from the meeting and thinking: 'I'll never vote for him.' But I would now. I've voted Liberal in the past, but I'll be voting for Powell at the next election.

I got very much the same story from Mr Holland, whom I interviewed shortly before the 1966 general election. (Mr Holland died in 1968.) He expressed a deep disgust at the apathy of his fellow citizens in their unwillingness to fight openly against immigration, and reserved particular venom for local

Conservatives, who, he said, with one or two exceptions, had done nothing to 'stop the flood'. Of both the town's M.P.s, in the early 1960s, Powell and Baird, Holland spoke with contempt. 'We tried to get their support,' he said. 'But they would have nothing to do with us.' Such a refusal to cooperate from Mr Enoch Powell was perhaps a little surprising, for the British Immigration Control Association called for nothing more than a ban on immigration, white and coloured. 'We are not,' said Mr Holland to the local Press when the local authority refused to let him a hall for a meeting 'a colour bar association.'

Despite the enthusiasm of the committee, however, and the regular monthly meetings, the Immigration Control Association's branch in Wolverhampton did not prosper. George Thomas admits:

We didn't have too big a following, really. People would bring their troubles to us, but when they were solved they went away, and they weren't too interested in meetings or anything like that.

The truth is that no anti-immigrant organization, still less an extremist right-wing or fascist political party has managed to get off the ground in Wolverhampton during the period of large-scale Commonwealth immigration into the area.

The British National Party, which by 1962 had got rid of Colin Jordan, and was growing in influence, never had more than a handful of members in Wolverhampton. Nor did Colin Jordan, whose base was in the West Midlands. Nor did the various Immigration Control Associations and Racial Preservation Societies which flourished in other parts of the West Midlands in the ensuing years. In the literature produced by such organizations for the whole of the 1960s, there is hardly a report from Wolverhampton. When, in 1966, the British National Party put up a candidate in Smethwick he was a Wolverhampton tool fitter, secretary of the Wolverhampton BNP branch who could not find enough support to stand in his own town.

The main reason for this can probably be traced to the entrepreneurial skilled-worker class background of Wolverhampton, which, while leading to greater individual prejudice, is staunchly suspicious of all organizations, particularly right-wing organizations. Part of the credit can go to John Baird, who conspicuously ignored possible electoral losses, and campaigned throughout for racial equality and tolerance. Even more goes to Geoffrey Ayre and his contacts in the local authority for the years of patient and careful welfare work. None of the credit, however, can go to Enoch Powell who treated all these developments with sublime indifference. The difference in attitude between Powell and Baird was startlingly demonstrated at a dinner in November 1960 of Jewish ex-servicemen, after which both M.P.s spoke. Baird used the opportunity to make a general onslaught on racialism indicating that the Jews and the Irish had lived 'a ghetto existence' in English cities, and that prejudice against the coloured citizens today was no less reprehensible than anti-Irish or anti-Semitic sentiment in the past. Powell, who spoke second, completely ignored such problems and spoke instead on behalf of Jews in modern society, explaining, perhaps significantly, that 'Jews are leaders in all fields of human endeavour, and as such I salute them.' (*Express and Star,* 14 November 1960).

This indifference to race relations in Wolverhampton persisted even after the 'monkey' had been caught and the Commonwealth Immigrants Act had been passed. The passing of the Act made little difference to the immigration figures. In the generally tolerant atmosphere following the legislation, the Conservative Government, with Powell in the Cabinet, continued to issue vouchers to prospective Commonwealth immigrants at the rate of some 40,000 a year. Dependants of immigrants already here, particularly of those who had rushed in to 'beat the Act', came in free of control. In the years 1962 to 1964, the number of coloured children in Wolverhampton schools, which caused such anxiety to Powell five years later, doubled – from 1,000 to 2,000 – without any complaint from him or any Conservative councillor.

Powell admits that, in the 'enormous relief' following the Bill, his interest in immigration control slackened. But there was no corresponding rise in his interest in race relations. From his argument about such lack of interest and concern in the years before control – that the crucial matter was to pass control legislation – it followed that, with the control act passed, he was free to apply his mind to the question of race relations and integration. In the event, Powell showed nothing but a high-minded disinterest in these matters. In 1965, a group of Wolverhampton councillors, Fabians and liberals founded the Council for Racial Harmony, one of the first such local bodies formed under the Labour Government. The organizers invited four hundred prominent people in the town to their opening rally, including the town's two M.P.s. From Mrs Renee Short, new Labour M.P. for the North East constituency, they received a letter in reply wishing them well. From Enoch Powell they received no reply at all. After the opening meeting, the organizers wrote again to the M.P.s inviting them to a meeting to discuss the setting up of an organization. Once more they received no reply from Enoch Powell. The original chairman, a Labour councillor called George Costley, says that Powell never involved himself in any way in this sort of activity. 'We did look for some leadership from Mr Powell' he says 'but it was not forthcoming. We had hoped he would put his weight behind us, but he didn't.'

In 1966, the Council for Racial Harmony became the Commission for Community Relations with a full-time Secretary. In 1968, Mr Aaron Haynes was appointed secretary and he wrote at once to both M.P.s suggesting a meeting. No reply was forthcoming from Powell until after the latter's sensational speech in Birmingham on 20 April 1968. Haynes met Powell some two weeks after this speech and was astonished at Powell's ignorance of the Committee and its work. The Committee had by that time been functioning with the help of government money for nearly two years, but Haynes remembers Powell asking how it was financed. 'It suddenly struck me, as we were talking,' said Haynes, 'that he didn't even know we existed until then.' Haynes then begged Powell to give him more information about the old lady, pestered by immigrants, to whom Powell had referred in his speech. Haynes assured Powell that he and his committee would do their utmost to smooth down tension in the street and relieve the old lady's plight. But Powell would give no information about the old lady and the Committee to this day have received no information which would enable them to help her.

The sample census of 1966 showed, in the enlarged borough of Wolverhampton, 12,700 people born in the main areas of coloured immigration to Britain – the West Indies, India and Pakistan. Allowing for the fact that the percentage in the old borough of Wolverhampton is marginally higher than this and that the figures do not include coloured people born in this country, this is still a small percentage compared with many other areas of immigrant settlement. Although some 13 per cent of children in Wolverhampton schools are coloured, this percentage is still a great deal lower than in many London boroughs of similar size. A detailed survey, covering some 524 interviews in Wolverhampton in the winter 1966–7 reported that:

With the partial exception of the work place, Wolverhampton residents reported more difficulties (with immigrants) than respondents from other boroughs.

The reasons for this, as outlined in the paper 'Race, the Politicians and Public Opinion' by Nicholas Deakin (delivered to the British Sociological Association, March 1969) vary from the class background of the area to the nature of the original immigration from rural and illiterate Jamaica. The important fact about the figures of heavier resentment however is that they are still, when compared with Mr Powell's grandiloquent generalizations, very small. The Deakin paper ends:

Perhaps the most striking of all the findings in the main study is the limited extent to which the respondents are concerned by the problems raised by immigration. Although, when invited to make an assessment of the situation, 49 per cent of the sample felt that local attitudes towards coloured people were less favourable than the national average, and 65 per cent (by far the highest level in any of the boroughs studied) felt that the situation was bound to deteriorate, when invited to assess the importance of the situation *to themselves as individuals* only 38 per cent of those questioned regarded the immigration issue as being important or very important. 43 per cent felt that it was a matter of no great importance, and 19 per cent that it was not important at all. It is against the background of these findings that the statement by one of the local Members (Enoch Powell) should be seen: 'For over ten years, from about 1954 to 1966, Commonwealth immigration was the principal and at times the only, political issue in my constituency.'

Can an issue which is neither the main preoccupation of the majority of local inhabitants nor one which finds expression through the orthodox channels of communication legitimately be described as the principal local political issue?

Dr George Jones, who sat on the Wolverhampton council throughout the period, has written a long and detailed study of local politics in the town (*Borough Politics: a study of Wolverhampton Borough Council*, Macmillan, 1969). The book devotes a chapter to the areas of political conflict in the town during the 1950s and early 1960s, and outlines everything which could conceivably have been regarded as a political issue in Wolverhampton. Throughout the 400 pages, there is no mention of immigration as a political issue.

Yet perhaps the most interesting reflection on Mr Powell's view that immigration was the 'principal and at times the only political issue' for over ten years, comes from Mr Peter Farmer, leader of the Conservatives on the Wolverhampton Corporation and for three years chairman of Enoch Powell's divisional Conservative Party. Farmer, a local bookseller, had been on the council for nearly twenty years, and knows perhaps more about local Conservative politics than anyone else in Wolverhampton.

I asked Farmer whether he thought immigration was a major issue in the town before he himself raised it in a question to the Chairman of the Health Committee in the spring of 1965.

'No, it wasn't,' he replied.

I think it took everyone by surprise – the fantastic speed with which the thing overtook the town. Up to then the numbers in the town were not enough to worry us.

Farmer described the amount of discussion and public concern about immigration in the year or two before 1965 as 'negligible, infinitesimal I would say.'

In 1960 and 1961, he remembered, there were 'various discussions in the Party about the Bill. But it was not a matter of public debate – rather of private discussion.' I asked Farmer finally whether he was saying that, until 1965, immigration was not a 'major, central issue affecting the town', and he replied, 'Yes, I think it would be fair to say that.'

It is a fair assumption that Peter Farmer is much closer to the reality than his Member of Parliament, and that Powell's characterization of immigration as 'the principal political issue in Wolverhampton over ten years is little more than a fabrication to avoid an awkward coincidence: namely that immigration became the principal political issue in Wolverhampton soon after it became a principal political issue in th speeches of Enoch Powell.

Again and again, in attempts to justify his sensational outbursts on immigration and race in 1968 and 1969, Enoch Powell has referred to the situation in his constituency. The identification of immigration as the main problem in his constituency throughout the 1950s and 1960s dates from the 1964 election, but is taken up with increasing enthusiasm as the months go on. Throughout, the picture is created of a man with close links with the people, springing from them, working and living with them, suffering their deprivations, their worries, and their frustrations. These 'natives' (as he described them) of Wolverhampton are pictured always in Powell's mythology as people whom he understands and who understand him.

'Acts of an enemy,' wrote Powell,

bombs from the sky, they could understand; but now, for reasons quite inexplicable, they might be driven from their homes and their property deprived of value by an invasion which the Government apparently approved and their fellow-citizens elsewhere viewed with complacency. Those were the years when a 'For Sale' notice going up in a street struck terror into all its inhabitants. I know; for I live within the proverbial stone's throw of a street which 'went black'. (*Daily Telegraph*, 7 February 1967).

In interview after interview about his attitude to immigration, Powell has repeated this theme. He lived, he said, in an area which was one of the first to come under West Indian occupation. And this was not even a traditional slum area, but an area which used in the good old days to house some of Wolverhampton's more respectable bourgeoisie.

Mr Powell does not live (in any meaningful sense of the word) within a stone's throw, or indeed within a few miles of streets which went black. He lives at No. 30 South Eaton

Place, London, SW1, in the heart of London's most fashionable residential area. The only black men seen in South Eaton Place are maharajahs, diplomats or, occasionally, dustmen. When a 'For Sale' notice goes up in South Eaton Place (which is rare, because Belgravia estate agents seldom stoop to such common practice), the inhabitants are not struck with terror. They muse instead on the sale price and on the increase in the value of their property, which has been on the uninterrupted increase for as long as estate agents there can remember.

What enables Powell to lay claim to living in the midst of all this terror is the fact that, unlike most of the constituents whose fears he claims to represent, he can afford two houses, and, from his earliest days in his association with Wolverhampton, he has had a house or a flat in Wolverhampton. His house in Merridale Road, which he bought in 1954 is indeed in an area where many of the West Indians first settled, but it is not his usual residence. He uses it as a convenient *pied-à-terre* in his constituency and spends several weeks a year there with his family. If he is struck down with terror at the sight of the streets around his Wolverhampton house 'going black', Mr Powell has a quick and easy escape route via the new highspeed British railways service, and in a matter of two and a half hours he can be safe again in Belgravia.

The truth is that Powell has never been a 'constituency M.P.'. When he jokingly told a Nuffield seminar in May 1967 that 'all M.P.s detest their constituents to a greater or less degree,' he was expressing part of the truth of his own political life and experience. Powell's work in his constituency is hard and conscientious, but it is confined very much to routine surgeries and visitations of new constituents. Moreover, unlike his former counterpart in Wolverhampton North East, John Baird, Powell has always kept political controversy in his constituency down to a minimum. Richard Reynolds, the Labour Party secretary in Wolverhampton South West since 1945, remembers Powell speaking at the traditional public political meetings at the Lych Gate in the 1950 and 1951 elections. 'After he got elected,' says Reynolds, 'he dropped public meetings like a shot. He hardly ever holds public meetings

in between elections. In fact I can hardly remember one.'
Desperate attempts by Labour and Liberal Parties to entice
Powell into public debate at election times have always failed,
and when in 1955 the Labour candidate took out a half page of
the local paper challenging Powell to answer Labour's case,
he was answered with a short four-line letter.

An interesting comparison in this context can be made between Powell and Mr Patrick Gordon Walker, former M.P.
for Smethwick. Gordon Walker was defeated in the 1964 election after a Conservative campaign which, among other things,
attacked Gordon Walker for being out of touch with Smethwick. Much fun was made of the fact that Gordon Walker
lived in Hampstead Garden suburb.

It was clearly true that Gordon Walker was not at home in
the company of the working people of the Black Country;
plainly true that he was an 'intellectual' who lived in Hampstead Garden Suburb, and preferred Hampstead Garden Suburb to Smethwick. Yet, in spite of all this, Gordon Walker
did maintain political contact and connexion with Smethwick.
The proof for that is in the local paper, the *Smethwick Telephone*, in which Gordon Walker wrote a political article almost every week for eighteen years. There is hardly an issue
of the unashamedly right-wing Conservative *Smethwick Telephone* which does not over those eighteen years contain some
reference to Gordon Walker in a political connexion.

Enoch Powell's record in Wolverhampton is quite different.
The *Wolverhampton Express and Star* is a daily paper with a
considerable reputation for thorough reporting. It is a right-
wing paper, though more mildly so than the *Smethwick Telephone,* and it gives considerable space to politics. Leafing
through the *Express and Star* over the years of Powell's being
an M.P., it is astonishing how little he is mentioned, and how,
when he is mentioned in a local context, it is in a frivolous or
'gossip' context. The number of political articles by Powell
in the paper over nearly twenty years are as many as Gordon
Walker wrote in Smethwick (in a weekly paper) in six months.
And the number of public meetings addressed by Powell on
political subjects, outside election times, are almost ten times
fewer than with Gordon Walker. The man from Hampstead

Garden Suburb, though his record was not outstanding, kept much closer political touch with his constituents than the man from Belgravia.

Throughout his political career, Enoch Powell has concentrated almost entirely on national issues. His speeches in Wolverhampton at election times have always dealt with the broad sweep of politics, hardly ever referring to local issues.

Even his contact with the local Conservatives on Wolverhampton Corporation was kept down to a minimum. In his book on Wolverhampton politics, Dr George Jones describes the formation in 1956 of a Conservative councillors' caucus, to meet regularly and discuss political initiatives.

'In 1956,' writes Jones,

the Conservative M.P. was invited to attend the caucus. He came, and was invited to attend whenever possible. In fact, he does not appear to have come again. (*Borough Politics: a study of Wolverhampton Borough Council* p. 193).

Powell has, throughout, presented an image of a distant, if conscientious Member of Parliament, concerned constantly with national issues whose speeches and writings were seen more as expressions of political theory than populist phraseology. In the years when he is out of the Government, his questions and speeches in Parliament seldom refer to Wolverhampton or its problems. He prided himself throughout all this on his reputation for thinking problems through on his own initiative, rather than mouthing the aspirations of others. His first-ever interviewer in Wolverhampton has concluded of Powell:

The first impression of him is that he prefers the logical argument to rousing the emotions. (*Express and Star*, 18 December 1949).

The characterization of himself as a man of the people, living and understanding their problems from association with them was entirely new and entirely false. It was, however, necessary, for in dealing with race and immigration Powell had decided to throw over his reputation for intellectual independence and rigour and adopt a populist posture on a swiftly-moving bandwagon.

Chapter 3
On the Bandwagon

'I have set and always will set my face like flint against making any difference between one citizen of this country and another on grounds of his origin.'

(Enoch Powell, writing in the *Wolverhampton Express and Star*, 10 October 1964).

'The West Indian or Asian does not by being born in England become an Englishman. In law he becomes a United Kingdom citizen by birth; in fact, he is a West Indian or Asian still.'

(Enoch Powell, speech at Eastbourne, 16 November 1968).

Enoch Powell's first signed, published reference to immigration was in a book review in the *Sunday Times* four months before the 1964 general election. The book reviewed was *The Economics of the Colour Bar* by W. H. Hutt which argues that the chief cause of discrimination in South Africa was 'central planning' in the South African economy. Powell warmed to this theme, and used it to attack the granting of aid to the underdeveloped countries. At the end of the article, he dealt with 'the live issue of immigration and coloured immigration in the United Kingdom'. He thought it 'arguable' that the rate of immigration before the Commonwealth Immigrants Act would have resulted in a 'less than corresponding increase in production'. But the real argument for control was, according to this review, that 'the United Kingdom and the Commonwealth do not constitute one community'. Within a 'community', free movement of labour is, wrote Powell, excellent. The movement of labour between 'communities' must be controlled.

The tone of the review was academic and mild, and, towards the end, Powell declared his faith in a multiracial society in Britain.

On the other hand, the immigrants who have come already, or who are admitted in the future, *are* part of the community. Their most rapid and effective integration is in the interests of all. Anything which tends to create a separate market for the labour and abilities of the immigrants prejudices the general interest as well as that of the immigrants themselves. Money is colour-blind, and economic forces will help the work of integration which must be done if a homogenous community, local and national, is to be restored. (*Sunday Times*, 14 June 1964).

Not surprisingly, perhaps, for so devoted a multiracialist, Powell scrupulously avoided joining the clamour for increased immigration control which preceded the 1964 election, though there were plenty of opportunities for him to do so.

On 23 July, a group of all but two of the Conservative M.P.s from Birmingham (the exceptions were Mr Aubrey Jones and Sir Edward Boyle) attended a meeting at the house of Mr Geoffrey Lloyd, a former Minister, and drew up a statement outlining their intention to 'run' the immigration issue during the election campaign. In the local elections the previous May, the Conservatives had taken control of the council at Smethwick, after winning three seats against the national 'swing' to Labour. The previous year, three of the five Tory local election gains in the entire country had been in Smethwick. No one in Smethwick doubted that the Tory gains could be accredited to the campaign which Mr Peter Griffiths, the Conservative candidate, had waged since 1962 for an almost complete ban on immigration. The Smethwick campaign and the Birmingham meeting were a considerable embarrassment to Conservative Central Office, whose policy directors let it be known that official Party attitudes strongly conflicted with those of Mr Peter Griffiths and of Mr Harold Gurden, M.P. for Selly Oak, who inspired the meeting in Birmingham. Central Office observers were sent to Smethwick to keep Griffiths under control during the election campaign, and most of the Birmingham M.P.s responded obediently to Central Office pleas to keep the issue off the hustings. The controversy raged all through the summer and autumn, taking up many inches of Press and television coverage, but never once was there a flicker of reaction from Mr Enoch Powell. No doubt he had made up his mind, as he had done in 1959, that the 'monkey' had to be caught softly once more.

In the spring of 1964, Smethwick had been plastered with

sticker cards on which were printed the slogan: 'If you want a nigger neighbour, vote Labour'. Griffiths and the Tories had denied responsibility for the stickers, but Griffiths had affirmed: 'I would not blame anyone who said that . . . it was,' he said, 'a manifestation of popular feeling.' (*The Times*, 13 October 1964).

On 24 September, the week before the election campaign started, readers of the *Wolverhampton Express and Star* discovered that stickers had been plastered up in Wolverhampton with the slogan;

Vote Labour for More Nigger-type Neighbours!

Mrs Renee Short, Labour candidate for Wolverhampton North East, responded, not surprisingly:

These are fascist tactics.

Enoch Powell, however, was more cautious:
'I have not seen nor heard of these,' he said.

I have not started my campaign yet. I am not adopted as candidate until tomorrow, so I am not making any comment or observation on anything at this stage.

By the 26th, after Powell had been adopted, the Tories' minds were made up:

Conservatives in the two Wolverhampton constituencies do not wish to become involved in the controversy about anti-Labour 'smear cards' circulating in the town. The cards state: 'Vote Labour for More Nigger-type Neighbours.'
Mr Enoch Powell said on Thursday that he could not comment till he had been formally adopted for the South West constituency. He was adopted last night.
His agent, Mr R. N. Pollard, said today:
'Mr Powell has had to go away for the weekend on a private matter, but I don't think he would want to comment. It is doubtful if we shall ever discover who is responsible for the cards. We have not seen any of these cards. They are not worth commenting on.' (*Express and Star*, 26 September 1964).

On 30 September, Powell went to speak at a meeting of the Conservative candidate for neighbouring Bilston, Mr John Oxford. Powell sat silently while Oxford treated his audience to a speech of which Peter Griffiths would have been proud:

'I can take you down to Stow Heath,' he offered, 'and what will you see? Fifty or sixty cars pulling up, a juke box blaring out music until three in the morning, and gambling and prostitution will be in evidence.' There was much more besides from Mr Oxford, but nothing of the kind from Mr Powell, who, according to the reports, made no reference to immigration in his speech. (*Express and Star,* 1 October 1964).

Powell's election address, published on 5 October, referred to immigration, as did almost every other Conservative election address in the Black Country – but the reference was mild:

Control of immigration is essential not only for the people of Britain but also for the immigrants themselves. . . . I am convinced that strict control must continue if we are to avoid the evils of a colour question in this country, for ourselves and for our children.

The following day, however, immigration had assumed considerable proportions:

'The biggest issue locally?' asked a local Press survey of the Black Country constituencies. 'Immigration say two of them, Mr Powell and Mr Lloyd. . . .' For years now, since the late 1950s in fact, discussions with people, whether about education, housing, pensions, employment, or other things always comes round to this topic, says Mr Powell. . . . It will be Mr Powell's business to show that the Conservative Government's action and policy on this has been the only sound and humane policy which is available. (*Express and Star,* 6 October 1964).

On this, the first occasion when Powell refers to immigration as 'the biggest issue' in Wolverhampton, he dates its predominance back to the 'late 1950s'. In later speeches and articles, he dated it from the 'early 1950s' or 'from 1954'. The statement and the passage in the election address, however, showed that Powell intended to raise this 'biggest issue' cautiously and in moderate language. Soundness and humanity are the themes. There is not a hint of a more restrictionist attitude towards immigration control. The Commonwealth Immigrants Act was quite enough.

Startling proof that Enoch Powell was not associated in any way with the campaign which Griffiths was waging in

Smethwick was a report in the *Observer* (4 October 1964), entitled, REBUFF FOR TORY AT SMETHWICK.

The Conservative candidate for Smethwick, Alderman P. H. S Griffiths, who is demanding an immediate ban on all immigration, has cancelled an invitation to Enoch Powell to speak on his behalf. Following this, I understand, Sir Edward Boyle has refused to speak for him.

Mr Powell's invitation was cancelled because the date previously agreed would be personally inconvenient for Alderman Griffiths. But it is widely assumed that Mr Powell, who is extremely hostile to bringing race into politics, was thought an embarrassment.

This 'assumption' is now hotly denied by Powell, who writes to me that the cancellation was 'owing to a double-booking'. I cannot trace the source of the 'assumption' but there can be little doubt that it accurately reflected Powell's reputation at the time. His spurning of the advances of Cyril Osborne in 1958–9; his record at the Ministry of Health and his austere and principled political demeanour had established him in the eyes of most political observers as 'extremely hostile to bringing race into politics'.

As the election campaign went on, however, the Smethwick controversy increasingly dominated the headlines. Almost everything Peter Griffiths said and did was reported in the local Press, with the result that Tory candidates in the area were constantly questioned about it. Letters appeared in the papers like the one from *Admirer,* which was printed in the *Express and Star* of 9 October:

My idea of an ideal M.P. is Mr Peter Griffiths, candidate for Smethwick. He is not afraid to speak his mind on coloured immigrants.

This was a bit hard on Enoch Powell who had been Admirer's M.P. for fourteen years. The day after the letter appeared, Powell proved that he too was not afraid to speak out on coloured immigrants. He wrote an article for the *Express and Star* (one of the very few he has written in twenty years association with Wolverhampton) which appeared together with a contribution on the same subject from a Labour M.P. (John Stonehouse) and a Liberal (Jo Grimond). Powell's article started so mildly that it was almost indistinguishable from the other two:

I have set and always will set my face like flint against making any difference between one citizen of this country and another on grounds of his origin.

I am certain that not only the Conservative Party but the overwhelming majority of people in this country are of the same mind and wish – this is what it amounts to – to see the coloured immigrants no less integrated into the life and society of what is now their homeland than any other group, such as the Jewish community or the thousands of Poles living in Britain today. No other prospect is tolerable.

There was, however, 'one condition' without which this could never be fulfilled: continued, tight control of immigration. Powell repeated the lie that 300,000 immigrants would have entered the country from the Commonwealth without control,[1] and pointed out that in 1963 50,000 immigrants came in. This was too many, but what was Powell to do about it? In the article's most interesting passage, Powell wrote:

As there is an inescapable obligation of humanity to permit the wives and young children of immigrants already here to join them, it follows that the rate of all other new admissions must be reduced further still.

In other words, the numbers coming in must be controlled by granting fewer vouchers to Commonwealth citizens wishing to come and work in Britain. Dependants should still be allowed to come in freely. Indeed, they should always be.

That, according to Enoch Powell, was 'an inescapable obligation of humanity'.

The *Express and Star* article was reprinted in the *Sunday Express,* but it was of little national political interest. Despite the specific recommendations for further labour voucher control the general tone of the article was so conciliatory, and the attitude of Wolverhampton Conservatives throughout the election so clearly opposed to Smethwick tactics that the Wolverhampton general election campaign in 1964 was nowhere regarded as comparable with that of Smethwick. Mr Eric Robinson, now Liberal candidate for the South West constituency, attended Powell's eve of poll meeting in Wolverhampton

1. The figure was based on the number of applications for vouchers which had not been granted. Only a percentage (about 65 per cent) of granted vouchers were taken up.

Grammar School, and was pleasantly surprised when a hostile question about immigrants in Wolverhampton was 'turned aside' by Powell 'as being in a non-political area' (Robinson's letter to me, 20 March 1969). Mr Tony Gardner, now M.P. for Rusholme, who was the Labour candidate for the Wolverhampton South West in 1964, outlines his own reactions at the time in a letter to me (3 April 1969):

I was adopted candidate for South West Wolverhampton in 1962, and frankly had no idea that Mr Powell was likely to raise immigration as an issue. Indeed, I cannot recall any comment from him during the lead-up to the General Election. Apart from the somewhat vague and rather disturbing passage in his election address, I do not recall that he raised the immigration issue to any substantial extent during the actual campaign. To sum up, Mr Powell pursued throughout the campaign his more normal if somewhat strange economic line and no one was more shocked than I was when he made his now famous speech. Until then, I had always regarded him as a rather weird right-winger in economic affairs with quite radical views on social issues.

This clearly was the view of the author of the section on Britain in the Institute of Race Relations' Monthly Newsletter for October 1964 who referred to Mr Powell's 'austerely objective views on the immigration issue'; and of the Labour Mayor of Wolverhampton, Councillor H. Bagley, who said at the first annual meeting of the Commonwealth Welfare Council after the election:

Wolverhampton has been fortunate to have avoided racial extremists during the election.

Even Geoffrey Ayre who always kept a hawk eye out for any racial transgressions concedes that there was not, in October 1964, any sign of the 'trigger mechanism' to spark off serious racial antagonisms of which he had warned seven years earlier.

Two developments, however, took place on polling day which had a considerable effect on Enoch Powell. First, the Conservatives were defeated and their Ministers and former Ministers faced a spell in opposition. The prospect of a spell in opposition filled Powell with exhilaration. Had the Conservatives won the 1964 election, Powell would have found himself in a difficult position. He had refused to serve under Sir Alec Douglas Home, because he regarded him a poor second best in the 1963 leadership struggle and because he was shocked at Home's cavalier rejection of his peerage. If Home had led the Tories back for a fourth term of office, Powell's judgement and future would have been at stake. As it was, Powell could claim he had been proved right. He could with some attempt at justification rejoin the Shadow Cabinet without compromising his principles. Above all, opposition gave him a chance to campaign in the open and to play politics as he had not been able to play it since the heady days when he was working out how to reconquer India.

'In this situation,' he told Peter Lewis of the *Daily Mail, a* fortnight after the election,

I find myself going back to first principles. We have pulled our punches on trade unionism.

We have pulled our punches on stating that free enterprise protects people and guarantees a fairness that no Government intervention can guarantee. You can't expect people to accept what you stand for unless you are uninhibited in defending it and propagating it. (*Daily Mail*, 29 October 1964).

Almost at once he discovered that the Tories had pulled their punches on another rather more delicate matter. In Smethwick, unlike anywhere else in the country, there had been a substantial swing to the Conservatives. The Foreign Secretary had lost his seat, and an entrenched Labour majority had been converted into a majority for Peter Griffiths. Griffiths's victory commanded the attention not only of the Prime Minister, the newspapers and television but of many thousands of Midland Conservative workers smarting with defeat. Many of them had pressed their candidates to raise the immigration issue. Many of them had disapproved of the 'gutless' approach of Conservative Central Office. These people had been proved right by the most important statistics of all – the voting figures. There could now be no doubt about it. A sustained and vigorous campaign for stricter controls on immigration could win votes. This fact drove many Conservatives off the fence and onto the immigration control bandwagon. Among those who made the move was Enoch Powell.

Writing in the *Sunday Times* on the Sunday after the election

Powell defended his raising the immigration issue at the election.

It is not colour prejudice or racial intolerance to say that only if substantial further addition to our immigrant population is now prevented will it be possible properly to assimilate the immigrants already here, which in turn is the only way to avoid the evils of the colour question. I said this in my own election address; I said it in speeches; I wrote it in the Press. . . . A politician who says these things does no more than his duty. (*Sunday Times*, 18 October 1964).

Powell wrote that he was

shocked by the sounds of self-righteous unction which arose after Alderman Peter Griffiths won the seat at Smethwick. I do not agree with people who say that the result is a disgrace.

Speaking in his constituency on the same theme that week-end, Powell again defended the Smethwick result, though he was still cautious about the Smethwick candidate. 'Mr Powell' reported the local paper 'made it clear that he was not supporting or defending Alderman Griffiths, but was supporting and defending his own line.' (*Express and Star*, 19 October 1964). A good explanation for this hesitancy about Griffiths personally was supplied by the post-election issue of the Liberal magazine, *New Outlook*. Griffiths's strategy, it suggested, would be to push his henchmen at Smethwick into Tory candidatures in the Midlands, thus 'setting out to round up the West Midlands'. The writer added that Griffiths faced a rival contender in Enoch Powell 'who has moved in advance for the right to lead any Tory block which springs up there.' (*Guardian*, 27 November 1964). From now on, in fact, though steering clear of the immediate lobby around Peter Griffiths, Enoch Powell was going to throw punches on immigration as on everything else.

Before long he was barnstorming around the country proclaiming the irrelevance of Empire (at Trinity College, Dublin) and the importance of denationalizing the Post Office (at Batley, Yorks.).

Meanwhile the two main parties, inside and outside Parliament, wrestled with the implications of Smethwick. The Conservative Party was split between the right wing clamouring for tighter immigration controls and 'radicals' like Mr Aubrey Jones, M.P. for Birmingham, Hall Green, who argued in the debate on the Expiring Laws Continuance Bill in November against further cuts in immigration on the grounds that the economy needed labour. Although most Conservative leaders favoured tighter controls, 'integration' was put high on the agenda for policy review in January 1965, and even the newly-formed Monday Club, in a document on immigration, urged the building of more hostels for single immigrants and the recruitment of coloured police. Firm orders went out from Conservative Central Office to their candidate in the Leyton by-election in December and January who had, before his campaign, made an interesting contribution about 'blacks coming in on banana boats', to hold off the immigration issue.

The pressure from below for a 'strong lead' on control was, however, irresistible, especially as the Labour Government, under cover of Ministerial speeches of horror about Smethwick, were scrambling to safeguard their position by enacting more controls. On 3 February, Sir Alec Douglas Home, the Tory leader, made a speech in Hampstead arguing for tighter control of immigration, a clamp-down on evasion and a Government scheme to assist immigrants who wanted to return home. Today, Enoch Powell claims some credit for 'persuading Alec Home to make that speech'. The following day, Sir Frank Soskice announced that the Government was issuing strict instructions to immigration officers to ensure that 'evasions' of the Act were stamped out. (These 'evasions' were purely fictitious: see, Peter Norman, 'Who is Guilty of Evasion?' I.R.R. Newsletter, November 1965). In Smethwick, Peter Griffiths and his henchmen continued with their policies, notably a plan for Marshall Street whereby the council would intervene to ensure that no more houses were bought by blacks.

On 5 February, Sir Cyril Osborne threw the leadership of his Party into confusion by placing a motion on the order paper calling for the banning of all future immigration into Britain except for those whose parents or grandparents were born in Britain. The Tory leaders approached Osborne plaintively, begging him to amend his motion and to argue for 'periodic and precise limits' on immigration. Sir Cyril Osborne obliged, and, when leave to move his Bill came before the Commons on 1 March, Sir Alec Douglas Home, the Tory leader, Mr Edward Heath, his successor, and Mr Enoch Powell, among other Shadow Cabinet Ministers, marched into Osborne's lobby.

Yet the Conservative Party leadership was still schizophrenic about immigration. Early in March, the Shadow Home Secretary, Peter Thorneycroft, made a speech at the Conservative Central Council strongly advocating more controls, and, in late March, led a debate on immigration stressing the importance of integration. The leadership was under pressure from its rank and file to continue demands for more control, and to some extent were forced to give way to these demands. Much of the leadership, however, did so reluctantly. The Party chairman, Edward Du Cann, argued on 15 March for 'some sort of pause in the argument to work out sensible solutions'. On 18 April, the *Sunday Express,* whose political correspondent was very close to the Conservative leadership, announced that if the Government did not cut back immigration, the Tories would make it an election issue. There was some anxious lobbying of the Government by more liberal Tory leaders, who argued, somewhat desperately, for more immigration controls so that the whole subject could be dropped. Unofficial pledges were made to the Government that, if drastic restrictions on immigration were imposed, the Conservatives would not raise the issue at the election. The prospect of such a silence was too juicy a bait for the Labour Government to ignore, and, by the beginning of May, it was clear that the Government would introduce further controls before the end of the summer session.

Throughout this period, Enoch Powell had thrown his influence in the Shadow Cabinet behind a 'strong line' on immigration. His name, however, was not yet publicly identified with restrictionism. He was still regarded as someone whose main concern was with economic issues and who was likely to devote most of his energies to his responsibilities as Shadow Minister of Transport.

Events in the Black Country, however, soon persuaded Powell to re-engage in the immigration controversy.

On 5 January 1965, the Medical Officer of Health for West Bromwich, Dr H. O. M. Bryant, issued an annual report which said among other things that the immigrant birth rate was remarkably high. 'The high birthrate among immigrants' wrote Dr Bryant 'is partly caused by the fact that most of them are young people.' This simple point that the enormous majority of immigrants were young, of working and of child-bearing age, and that therefore a percentage comparison of their birth rate with that of the indigenous population was meaningless, appeared to have satisfied people in West Bromwich, where Dr Bryant's report was greeted with total silence.

Three months earlier, in October 1964, Dr J. F. Galloway, Medical Office of Health for Wolverhampton, had issued his annual report for 1963 in which he stated that Commonwealth immigrants had 'produced 22·7 per cent of all births and accounted for 30·4 per cent of hospital confinements' – a fact which Dr Galloway also attributed, though rather less clearly, to the age group of the immigrants.

Dr Galloway's report was not noticed by local politicians when it was published. Some four months later, however, when immigration had become a major political issue, it was pounced on by Wolverhampton Conservatives, notably their leader on the council and the chairman of the South West constituency association, Mr Peter Farmer. On 22 March, Farmer asked a question of the chairman of the Council's Health Committee about the coloured birth rate, and was greeted with cries of 'Smethwick!' Mr Farmer did not get an answer to satisfy him, and he pursued the matter. With other Tory councillors, he organized a plan of action, based on propaganda about the likelihood of 'a black majority' in Wolverhampton in the near future. The *Daily Telegraph* of 19 April reported:

Councillor Peter Farmer heads a group of Tory councillors who intend to draw the attention of Mr Enoch Powell, Conservative M.P. for Wolverhampton South West, to the implications of the (Galloway) Report.

Councillor Farmer then announced that he intended to ask an official question on the coloured birth rate, and achieved extensive advance publicity for his question. The *Birmingham Post* of 30 April had him saying:

It seems to me that places like Wolverhampton with high immigrant birth rates, could find themselves with white minorities within a quarter of a century.

Farmer asked his question on 3 May, and discovered that in 1964, 24 per cent of the births in Wolverhampton had been to coloured mothers (a not very surprising percentage considering that about a fifth of the people of child-bearing age in Wolverhampton were coloured).

'The figures,' he said,

do indicate that there should be no further immigration in our area if the local traditional culture is to be preserved.

Mr Farmer had just had an interview with Mr Powell, and he was very confident that 'the Conservatives will press strongly that the Government should tighten up the control on immigration.' (*Daily Telegraph,* 4 May 1965).

Whatever transpired in that interview between Farmer and Powell, the latter was clearly impressed. Discussions in the Shadow Cabinet had revealed to him the dilemma of the leadership and, in the situation of the spring of 1965, with the Government making noticeable advances across a broad front, the subject of immigration opened up admirable opportunities for 'unorthodox' opposition. In May, Powell travelled to Wolverhampton to speak to a group of Conservative women in his constituency, from whom he could expect little disagreement. (This, and all his subsequent 'controversial' speeches about immigration were made to carefully-picked audiences of the Tory faithful or of specially-invited guests who could not, in good manners, answer back).

The speech received considerable publicity, notably from the *Daily Mail*, whose main headlines read: 'POWELL'S SEND THEM HOME PLAN'. What was new to Tory Party policy in Powell's speech was the demand that Commonwealth immigrants be treated the same as aliens:

The Government is fiddling about with irrelevancies about the ownership of steel and land, while the urgent necessity of a change in the Immigration law remains unattended to. ... It is wholly absurd that while entry of aliens whether from France or China is controlled and policed with the utmost efficiency and permission to work and, even more, to settle is granted only with the greatest care and circumspection, Commonwealth immigrants still stream in with little surveillance and an absolute right to bring or fetch an unlimited number of dependants. ... These immigrants from the Commonwealth should be subject to the same considerations, controls and conditions as people from anywhere else. (*Sunday Mercury*, 21 May 1965).

This proposal contained one serious implication, which was not spelled out and was hardly noticed. Conservative Party policy at that time was that dependants of immigrants already in Britain had an absolute right of entry, free of control. Dependants then included spouses, children up to the age of eighteen and parents over the age of sixty. No one had explained this official Conservative line better than Enoch Powell in his 9 October statement, when he wrote that there was an 'inescapable obligation of humanity' to allow in these dependants free of control.

The free right of entry for dependants was written into the Conservative Commonwealth Immigrants Act of 1962 which first controlled immigrants from the Commonwealth. This was one of the major differences between that Act and the Aliens Act of 1919, by which foreigners entering Britain were controlled. The Aliens Act was passed in a fit of post-war xenophobic hysteria as a sop to the 'Hang the Kaiser' lobby when all foreigners entering Britain were regarded as possible spies or, at best, degenerate undesirables. The philosophy behind the Act had been outlined by Lloyd George who had said, while electioneering in the 1919 election, that foreigners were going to be 'fired out of the country'.

The Commonwealth Immigrants Act, by contrast, was introduced in an atmosphere of guilt and bad conscience by a Conservative Party which felt that Commonwealth immigration control was a dirty, if necessary, trick to play on the Empire. Its sponsors took the view that men and women exploited by British imperialism should be treated better than men and women exploited by any other form of imperialism. Commonwealth immigrants were seen, therefore, not as spying aliens, but almost as human beings.

The second consideration in the minds of the sponsors of the Act was the information which had already been collected by the Government about the areas of immigrant settlement. This information was, at the time of the Act, still pitifully small, but there was one theme common to all reports which not even the arch-restrictionists in the Home Office could answer: the beneficial aspects for race relations in areas of immigrant settlement when the immigrant workers were joined by their families. These had been noticed by all local authorities where the problem had arisen and particularly so in the Midlands. (See chapter 1).

The Aliens Act had not allowed the 'right' of an admitted alien to bring in any of his family. Immigration officers sometimes allowed in such dependants, but they were as much subject to the immigration controls as the original immigrants.

The evidence presented to the sponsors of the Commonwealth Immigrants Bill, however, of the advantages of dependants and of basing Commonwealth immigration policy on integration through the family unit, was so powerful that the Conservative Government, already prejudiced in favour of Commonwealth immigrants because of their imperialist past, agreed to write into the Act an unequivocal right of entry for immigrants' spouses and children under eighteen. This right was owed, as Powell had put it, 'out of an inescapable obligation of humanity'.

The words 'inescapable obligation' tend to give the impression of an obligation which cannot be escaped. The words of politicians, however, must not always be taken glibly at face value. 'Inescapable obligation', in modern politicians' language, can be taken, in normal circumstances, to mean: an obligation to humanity which cannot be escaped unless there are a large number of votes to be gained by escaping it.

Enoch Powell's reputation before he took a public interest in immigration, however, was that of a politician who did not use words or make pledges in the carefree manner which is associated, for instance, with Harold Wilson. Many of his past speeches and articles are cluttered with an almost pedantic obsession with logical explanation and formalistic argument. In his Wolverhampton speech on immigration in May 1965, however, he escaped from his inescapable obligation without explaining why and even without explaining that he had so escaped. The proposal that Commonwealth immigrants should be treated equally as aliens sounds harmless enough, until it is specified, which it nowhere is in Powell's speech, that this means that the wives and young children of immigrants are not allowed to come in free of control. Although that was the inevitable consequence of Powell's proposals, he did not have the courage to state it openly, and thus contrived to get publicity for his speech without being openly denounced by his Party leaders for transgressing Party policy.

Why had Powell changed his mind on dependants? Fortunately, we have an explanation from Powell himself. In March 1969, I was one of a team of three which interviewed Powell in the Tyne Tees television programme, 'Face the Press'. The following exchange took place between myself and Powell:

Q. In 1964 you wrote an article in the *Wolverhampton Express and Star* in which you said, among other things, that humanity demanded that the dependants of immigrants already here should be allowed in. Now you are saying, I understand, that dependants shouldn't be allowed in.

POWELL: Certainly.

Q. Has humanity changed?

POWELL: Yes, certainly it has. The balance of humanity has changed or at least I have certainly learnt more than I knew in 1964. Way back in 1956, I was urging my colleagues in Government that that fundamental change in the law of this country which would alone allow immigration control was vitally necessary. But I admit, and I can give you other quotations from 1963 to 1964 to prove it, that in 1963 and 1964 I did regard the million, approximately, of immigrants who were in this country, as more or less of the total problem. What I have realized – blame me if you like for not having realized it earlier, I'll accept the blame – what I have realized since is that that is only the lesser part of the problem, and when I have learnt (the facts were not available in 1964) that in 1964 already, in my own constituency a quarter of the births were immigrant births and they have been every year since. Then I have learned what I did not know five years ago, which I admit I ought to have known, and that is that the then million whom I have said over and over again over the years we could cope with, was only the lesser part of the problem and, if that is so, then anything which adds to the future growth in numbers – and particularly dependants coming to this country continuing to come, must do so, must especially do so, comes to be seen in a different light.

The picture which Enoch Powell presents of himself here is of a man who knew in 1964 that there were a million immigrants in this country (and that 10 per cent of his constituency population was immigrant), believed that Britain could 'deal with' this problem, and therefore described it as an inescapable obligation of humanity that the million or so here already should be joined by their wives and small children.

Then, in 1965, this same Enoch Powell suddenly realized that the million immigrants already here were 'the lesser part of the problem'. He was confronted with the startling and probably rather disgusting fact that these black people, when they mingle together in wedlock, produce children. To use a biblical expression, they multiply. And the arrival in this country of immigrants' wives from abroad led, astonishingly, to an increase in the births of black children. In Wolverhampton it led to the wholly unforeseeable situation where a quarter of the child-bearing population produced a quarter of the number of children. These 'facts' had not been available before 1964, and Mr Powell had not been appraised of them. That was why he declared it as an inescapable obligation of humanity to allow in wives and children. As soon as he discovered that these wives would produce more children, and that the problem would therefore increase, he concluded that 'humanity had changed' as had its obligations.

Powell pins this explanation to the pretext that 'the facts' about immigrant births in his constituency were 'not available' in 1964. Powell expanded on this theme in his speech at Wolverhampton on 9 June 1969:

In Wolverhampton, we have a remarkable series of figures, extending back to 1963. ... We have these figures because in that year, the

82

Medical Officer of Health gave instructions that the place of the birth of the mother should be inserted on every birth card. 'It takes five years to get rid of a Medical Officer of Health' he explained to me 'and I was then coming up to five years to retirement.' Statistics in this form, of course, make it possible to identify the proportion of births attributable to mothers from the new Commonwealth.

This notion that the first available figures about Commonwealth births in Wolverhampton were given in 1964 (in Galloway's Report for 1963) is also held by Dr Galloway, who told me that he printed the figures for Commonwealth births in his 1963 Report because that was the first year when the figures from the 1961 Census were available and this made it possible for him to compare statistics about births with statistics from the Census of overseas-born population. I asked Dr Galloway whether he had made any reference to immigrant births in any of his reports before 1963, and he replied: 'No, I'm sure I didn't.'

The actual reports, however, tell a different story. In his annual Report for as far back as 1960, Dr Galloway had written:

An increasing proportion of the maternity beds available for normal cases are being occupied by recent immigrants whose housing accommodation makes it undesirable for a confinement in the home. Although they probably represent about 3 per cent of the population they provide over 25 per cent of admissions to maternity beds on social grounds...

In his Report for 1961, Dr Galloway wrote:

In 1961, about 30 per cent of admissions on social grounds for confinements came from approximately 3 per cent of the population who are recent immigrants.

Dr Galloway's 1963 figures which were startling enough to change Enoch Powell's mind about the right of entry of dependants showed that 30.4 per cent of hospital births were to immigrant mothers – exactly the same percentage as Dr Galloway had estimated publicly two years earlier. Enoch Powell had attributed his conversion about dependants to the fact that 'the facts were not available'. In fact, they had been available for three years in the official Health Report for the Borough.

Nor were Dr Galloway's Reports the only source of information available to Powell from which he could find out the facts about immigrant births. As Minister of Health, he received a large number of deputations from local authorities all over the land complaining about the 'strain' on maternity services caused by immigration. A report in the *Guardian* (20 December 1960) said that the Wolverhampton Health Committee was 'to approach Mr Powell about the influx of overseas immigrants' and argue for control of Commonwealth Immigration (though Mrs Ruby Illsley, then chairman of the borough's health committee, does not remember any such meeting).

Powell was constantly reminded, both from his constituency and as Minister of Health, of the problems associated with immigration, particularly the shortage of maternity beds. On 1 April 1963, Mr John Baird, M.P. for Wolverhampton North East asked in the House of Commons of the Minister of Health

if he is satisfied that the number of hospital beds for maternity cases in Wolverhampton is adequate; and if he will make a statement on the steps he is taking to improve the situation.

To which Powell replied that he was not satisfied, and that

plans are well advanced for a new maternity unit of 146 beds at New Cross. Meanwhile, thirteen more beds were opened last year at the Women's Hospital, and additional delivery rooms will shortly be provided.

There was perhaps no one who knew more about the problems created in the health service by immigration than Enoch Powell. The suggestion that he was unaware that the immigrant community was reproducing at a faster rate than the indigenous community, or that he was unable to work out that that process is inevitable in any immigration by family unit, attributes to Powell as a naïveté and a stupidity which he does not deserve.

The truth was that Powell's conversion to the case for immigration control of dependants was due not to 'new facts' available from the Wolverhampton Health Department, but to a shrewd appraisal of the political situation. The Conservative Party leaders were under great pressure from the rank and file to demand stricter immigration control. Even in Parliament, the lobby for such a campaign was gathering strength. In May, moreover, the figures for the second full year after the 1962 Act had been published, and they showed a sharp rise in the 'net' Commonwealth immigration, from 66,000 to 75,499. The rise, however, was not so much in the numbers of immigrant men (most of whom had come in with labour vouchers, and were therefore subject to control under the Act) but in women, from 20,017 to 27,768; and children, from 12,970 to 24,223. A glance at the figures indicated that further demands for control, if relevant, would have to be directed against dependants as well as against voucher-holders. The figures showed that ruthless control of voucher-holders would not make a decisive impact on immigration figures, nor would its effect be immediately noticeable in the figures for two or three years. According to the Press, further control of voucher-holders was already likely to be introduced. Until Powell spoke out at Wolverhampton, no one except the extreme right wing led by Osborne and Gurden had called specifically for a ban on dependants. Even Powell's speech was not specific. Not one of the reports of Powell's speech mentioned the fact that Powell, in sharp contrast to the Shadow Cabinet, was, in effect, calling for a control of dependants which went much further than Home's demand at Hampstead to 'include the number of dependants in the total number allowed in'. This was merely a restatement of the right of dependants to enter uncontrolled, but a plea to include the number likely to enter in before making an assessment of how many to include. Powell, on the other hand, was calling for the removal of the right of families to join immigrants.

Peter Thorneycroft's speech in the House of Commons in April had been quite specific on the family question. 'Close dependants' he had said 'have an absolute right of entry, and we on this side have no intention of preventing them in any way.' This policy came under close review in the special

Conservative Party policy committee, chaired by Mr Selwyn Lloyd. In a statement on 3 July, which Mr Lloyd disingenuously presented as his 'personal point of view', he argued for a 'one in, one out' immigration system, in which the Government allowed in immigrants according to the number who left the country. The Lloyd proposals clearly meant a ban on families as well as labour vouchers. A report in the *Guardian* of 9 July indicated that 'leading Conservatives' were very anxious to correct the impression that dependants were included in the 'one for one' proposals. Meanwhile, Sir Cyril Osborne called twice in July for an end to immigration – in neither case supported by Mr Powell.

In the last week of July and the first week in August, there were two important developments. The first was the resignation of Sir Alec Douglas Home and the election of Mr Edward Heath as Conservative leader by the Parliamentary Conservative Party. The second was the August White Paper in which the Government introduced further controls on immigration.

The first is important because of the candidature in the leadership election of Enoch Powell. From the outset the Press treated the Powell candidature as the gesture of a maverick. Powell, however, does little in politics just for fun, and there can be little doubt that he regarded his candidature as a serious challenge. Throughout the year, he had persisted, in spite of his position in the Shadow Cabinet, in making speeches which were clearly designed to set the Party alight. In February, he wrote an article for the *Director* appealing to industrialists not to cooperate with the Labour Government – an article which drew angry rebukes from the chairman of the British National Export Council (set up by Edward Heath) and the British Employers' Confederation and which seriously embarrassed the business-orientated elements in the Tory leadership. Later in the month, he made a speech to Conservative women at Aylesbury, calling for fresh ideas for Tory policy, and a snapping of the 'umbilical cord' binding the Party to 1951 (among the evils listed in this speech, incidentally, were 'laws which perpetuated the privileges of restrictionism in labour, brains and skill' – which was believed not to be a reference to the immigration laws).

In early March, he made another speech to the Young Conservatives conference in Folkestone pouring scorn on the Government's (and, in particular, Mr George Brown's) export promotion methods. This, again, greatly embarrassed those Tory leaders, Edward Heath in particular, who liked to associate themselves with export drives. On 4 April, the *Sunday Express* printed an article by Denis Thomas, entitled 'The Buttoned-Up Buccaneer Stirs Up the Tories' – a flattering profile of Enoch Powell, who was described as 'the man who has set himself the task of making the word "Conservative" not just respectable, but dynamic'. The article listed Powell's various resignations, and concluded:

Right or not, he cannot afford much longer to make a career of eating political berries in the wilderness. If it's power he's after, the place to seek it is in the party machine. And after that in Downing Street.

This propaganda had its effect, and when a handful of Powell's Midland colleagues in Parliament urged him to stand in the leadership election, he agreed. The result of the election, which gave Heath 150 votes, Maudling 133 and Powell 15 was a severe reminder to Powell that Tory politics were still firmly in the centre. The election of Heath must have depressed Powell considerably, for Heath represented all that Powell most distrusted in the new Conservatism. The suspicion of tradition and form, the worship of technocracy and statistics, a firm belief in the role of the State as the guider and supplier of modern monopoly capitalism – all these were alien to Powell's conception of a grand conservatism based on untrammelled private enterprise. Despite his immediate promotion by Heath to Shadow Minister of Defence (surely one of the most ham-fisted appointments ever made), Powell determined to continue all the more vigorously his campaign to 'make the word Conservative dynamic' and to jolt the Shadow Cabinet out of its centrism.

In this campaign there was, however, one issue on which he had started, tentatively, to make speeches which now afforded him few opportunities: immigration. Only four days after Heath's appointment, the Government published a White

Paper on Immigration from the Commonwealth. The document was ostensibly the result of the mission by Lord Mountbatten to various Commonwealth countries in an entirely unsuccessful effort to 'persuade' these countries that immigration from them to Britain had to be curbed. The controls recommended fell within the scope of the Commonwealth Immigrants Act (save certain proposals for deportation, which were eventually dropped). The number of work vouchers to be issued each year to Commonwealth countries, said the White Paper, would not exceed 8,500, which meant, in effect, that no more than 5,000 workers would come in. Moreover, all these workers would be skilled or would have a job of some importance to come to. Spouses and children under sixteen would still be allowed to join their heads of family already here. The severity of the controls was greeted with astonishment. Few had believed that the Labour leaders would go so far in 'tightening up' an Act which, three years earlier, they had strenuously opposed. There was criticism of the White Paper from the Liberal Party, from immigrant organizations, from a large number of Labour backbenchers and from the Bow Group. Though there was no time to debate the White Paper in the Commons before the summer recess, several Conservative M.P.s made known their opposition.

Perhaps as a result of an agreement with the Government, the Conservative Party reacted to the controls by silencing those of their supporters who wanted more controls and effectively dropping the issue of control from Party controversy. After the August controls, the 'liberals' in the Tory Party who believed with their chairman, Edward Du Cann, in 'looking for sensible solutions' began to dominate the immigration debate. M.P.s like John Hunt (Bromley), Humphry Berkeley (Lancaster), Norman St John Stevas (Chelmsford), Bernard Braine (South East Essex) and Richard Hornby (Tonbridge), began to make increasingly confident speeches arguing for integrative measures, now that 'realistic' controls had been imposed. Shortly before the Conservative Conference, the Bow Group published a pamphlet by Christopher Brocklebank Fowler advocating a 'positive attitude' to integration and outlining a series of proposals. The Bow Group

Quarterly, Crossbow (October–December 1965), contained an article by Malcolm Rutherford attributing the spiral of demands for immigration control in the Labour and Conservative Parties to the Smethwick result, demanding an end to the silence of benevolent liberals and calling on the Tory Party to return to its pre-Smethwick position of restrained moderation. The Young Conservative paper, *Impact* (Autumn 1965) came out for a national policy for integration and against racial prejudice and discrimination. Even Sir Gerald Nabarro, a man not normally associated with the party's liberal wing, called on his Party to treat the immigrants in this country 'as Englishmen, as neighbours, as friends, as comrades and colleagues'. (*Gloucester Citizen*, 25 September 1965).

This liberal ascendancy was reflected at the Conservative Conference at Brighton in October, where the mildest of all the thirty-one resolutions on immigration was chosen for debate. The motion made no reference to further controls, except to accept those already imposed, and called for

positive and wide-ranging measures for the integration of existing immigrants in the fields of housing, education, employment and the social services, backed by the generous resources of the Central Government.

The motion was moved by the author of the Bow Group pamphlet, Christopher Brocklebank Fowler, and was recommended to the conference by the Shadow Home Secretary, Peter Thorneycroft, who said that it exactly embodied Tory policy. Thorneycroft warned of the importance of remaining 'one nation' and said that, although Britain could not be a magnet to the whole world, immigrants once here should be treated as 'citizens of no mean city'.

The *Sun* optimistically summed up the debate as follows:

The taint of Smethwick and colour-prejudice was officially and effectively rubbed out of the Party record during a debate on immigration.... It was rubbed out by the hisses which greeted a solitary speech calling for a complete ban on immigration. (*Sun*, 15 October 1965).

The speech came from a Mr Reginald Simmerson, representing, suitably, the London University Graduates Association, who declared that 'to allow immigrants in is madness, but to allow coloured immigrants in is double madness'. Mr Simmerson was booed, and those who supported him had a bad conference. Indeed, such was the atmosphere in the Conservative Party that leading members of it could be found openly attacking the Labour Government's Immigration White Paper for being too restrictive. In a speech to the North Paddington Young Conservatives, Mr Christopher Chataway, M.P. for North Lewisham, declared:

We now find that the Labour Government have imposed a *greater increase of restrictions than the Conservatives wanted*. I feel that they should concentrate on improving conditions in the areas hit by the influx of immigrants. (*Kilburn Times*, 31 November 1965).

This view was not shared by Enoch Powell who returned to the subject in a speech in Birmingham on 21 November.

'Even after the August controls were enforced,' he said,

there was an inflow of over 10,000 from the West Indies and the Indian sub-continent alone in August and September. Such a rate of inflow is still far too high to be acceptable. It will not be got right until admission for aliens and Commonwealth immigrants is on the same basis...

'We should not,' he added, almost as an afterthought,

lose sight of the desirability of achieving a steady flow of voluntary repatriation for the elements which are proving unsuccessful or unassimilable. (*The Times*, 22 November 1965).

This speech was not widely publicized, but it earned for Powell his first public recognition as a leading anti-immigration propagandist. In the debate in the House of Commons on the renewal of the Immigration Act under the Expiring Laws Continuance Bill two days later, two Labour M.P.s singled out Powell's speech for special rebuke. Mr Roy Hattersley, M.P. for Sparkbrook, pointed out that Birmingham was

more in need of additional workers than any other place in the Commonwealth ... all the economic arguments are in favour of immigration.

And, in a bitter speech late at night, Mr Norman Buchan, M.P. for West Renfrew came even closer to the point:

(Mr Powell) says we cannot plan industry, we cannot plan our economy, we cannot plan an incomes policy – that is far too difficult and complex. We must leave it to the market. But he says we can plan human beings, the most complex and intricate of things. . . . Even our sea-green incorruptible, the right hon. member for South West Wolverhampton, is swinging onto this immigration bandwagon. (Hansard, 24 November 1965).

Inside the Conservative Party, the Powell Birmingham speech was greeted with only faint disapproval. Powell had irritated the Party leadership much more seriously at the Conservative Party Conference that year with a speech on defence, for which he was Shadow Minister, in which he cast doubt on the efficacy of maintaining a British presence in the Far East. The speech seemed to please the delegates, but caused angry rumblings among Tory backbenchers when the Press headlined the references to the Far East. Sir Alec Douglas Home issued a mild corrective to the effect that no British military withdrawal could be contemplated in conditions which would lead to a 'vacuum of power in any area which would be filled by a greedy aggressor'. On 30 October Mr Aidan Crawley, M.P. for Derbyshire West, launched a bitter personal attack on Powell, which was well received by a number of backbenchers, and, when Parliament was recalled, the Tory Parliamentary Party's defence and foreign affairs committee met on 10 November. A number of traditionalist backbenchers attacked Powell for his conference speech and demanded assurances that the Tory leadership were not contemplating a withdrawal East of Suez. 'Mr Powell was on the mat' wrote *The Times* political correspondent on 15 November 'and apparently did not enjoy it.' Yet another attempt to swing the Tory Party towards a new, 'dynamic' conservatism had failed and Powell came out much the worse from the exchange. If he was chastened by the experience, it did not alter his determination to proceed with unorthodox propaganda to shake the Party out of its theoretical lethargy.

For this purpose, the call for more immigration controls was clearly hopeless. Powell's Birmingham speech had failed to strike a spark of interest or enthusiasm in the Tory Party. By now, Conservative Party policy was firmly set on the road to 'integration' and, in the wake of the August White Paper, it was considered bad taste and bad politics to demand further controls.

This attitude continued into 1966. At the crucial Hull by-election in January, the Conservative candidate was Mr Toby Jessell who had not scrupled to raise the immigration issue in strident terms during the 1964 election, when he was a candidate for Peckham. Jessell suggested to Central Office that he might do the same in Hull, but Central Office were adamant that he should not do so.

Jessell obeyed his orders, and the issue did not arise. Central Office persevered with and even hardened their attitude. As the general election approached, despite some attempts by the Press to anticipate if not create immigration as a relevant issue, most experts agreed, rightly, that there was little political sting left in it. The August controls and the concern in both major parties with 'integrative' Government measures, coupled with the initial successes of the Labour Government in other fields removed the issue from electoral controversy. In January, Mr Peter Griffiths called for an 'absolute ban' on immigration and was followed by Alderman George Hawkins (candidate for West Bromwich) and Sir Gerald Nabarro with similar demands, but these were cries in the wilderness. The Conservative approach, despite an ambiguous section in the Party's manifesto for the March general election, which called for a 'vetting system' by which potential immigrants would be asked to state before they came how many dependants intended to join them later, was well summarized by the Party chairman, Edward Du Cann, as making 'particular reference to the assimilation of newcomers into the social fabric'. (*The Times*, 2 March 1966).

The Times' political correspondent reported on 7 March that 'Conservative candidates generally were reporting that the climate of opinion in the country had markedly improved since the controls were imposed' and David Loshak of the *Daily Telegraph* wrote a full series on the subject of the immigration issue in the general election, concluding that 'nearly all parties are anxious to damp down racial issues, in places even by tacit agreement between the parties'. (*Daily Telegraph*,

5 March 1966). Even in Smethwick, Mr Peter Griffiths raised the immigration issue as only the fourth and last of his main campaign points.

An exception to this rule seemed possible in Wolverhampton, where, at the start of the election campaign, a debate had been staged at St Luke's School between Mr Joe Holland, chairman of the Wolverhamption branch of the defunct British Immigration Control Association, who had sat for a year on the Corporation as a Conservative candidate, and Alderman H. E. Lane, leader of the majority Labour group. The local paper reported that

a crowded and often rowdy meeting confirmed that the explosive topic of immigration will be one of the major issues in this month's elections. ... There are still plenty of votes to be won by taking a firm line on immigration. (*Express and Star*, 4 March 1966).

Mr Holland stood as an anti-immigration Independent in the local borough elections which took place on 17 March, a fortnight before the general election, polled 1,175 votes, some 27 per cent of the total vote, and was beaten by the Conservative by only 400 votes. Holland's chief associate on the council, a Conservative, topped the poll, gaining substantially more votes than other Conservatives, in a ward in the heart of Mr Enoch Powell's constituency.

Until this time, apart from a brief passage in his election address, Mr Powell had made little or no reference to immigration in his campaign. The main issues, he told an election meeting at Warstones School on 2 March, were Rhodesia, Defence, Crime, Land Prices, Pensions, the railways, the stopgo economics of the Labour Government and the Common Market. Of what he later called 'by far the biggest political issue in Wolverhampton for the last ten years', there was no mention.

Two days later, the *Economist* expressed the view that 'Wolverhampton may be the town with the most to fear from political exploitation of anti-immigration feeling'. The *Economist* referred to Holland's vote, the close-knit nature of the immigrant community and its rural background. (*Economist*, 25 March 1966). The article was publicized in the local paper.

The following day, Enoch Powell made a speech at St Jude's School which was devoted almost entirely to immigration.

'All our efforts,' he said,

at integration will be swept away if the tide of new immigrants continues to flow in. The rate is still far too high.

At the present rate, he argued, there would be two and a half million immigrants in this country by the year 2,000.

An addition of that magnitude is an appalling prospect which would render the social and human problem we have already wellnigh insoluble. . . . Indeed, for my part, and speaking as one who has represented one of the areas affected, I believe that there would be no small benefit in a period of years during which the inflow and outflow were roughly balanced.

Once again, Powell's speech dwelt upon the question of integration and made it clear that his remedy ('one in, one out') was made 'for my own part' and not by his Party. Once again, there was no specific recommendation about dependants, though the logic of this speech was that they, too, should be controlled. In 1964, Powell wrote that he would 'always set his face like flint' against making any distinction between immigrants already here and the indigenous community. Now, once more, he was 'resolutely determined that the immigrants already here should have the same rights and the same treatment as anyone else'. On repatriation, which he had not mentioned in 1964, he stuck firmly to his Party brief, saying that 'help should be given to those who voluntarily wish to return home, and I stress the word voluntary . . . there can be no question of any kind of duress or compulsion'. (*Express and Star*, 26 March 1966).

The best comment on this intervention came from the Institute of Race Relations Newsletter, (May 1966):

Mr Enoch Powell, the Conservative candidate, devoted an entire speech to the issue. While advocating even stricter control, he did not attempt to whip up popular support on the subject. Nevertheless, his determined insistence that the subject should be a major issue perhaps showed a half-hearted desire to attract a few uncommitted votes.

As though to prove the point, Powell had told his eve of poll meeting:

The central question which is to be decided at this election is whether for the next five years we will be governed by fears or by realities. (*Daily Telegraph*, 31 March 1966).

When the votes were counted, Powell's majority had been cut by 3,271, and the swing to Labour in his constituency was 3.9 per cent, slightly lower than in Wolverhampton North East, and substantially lower than nationally. In Smethwick, Mr Peter Griffiths was swept off the political map in a swing of more than 7 per cent, resulting in a Labour majority of 3,490. Everywhere, the story was the same. Mr Brian Walden, the Labour M.P. for All Saints, Birmingham, in whose constituency is one of the largest immigrant concentrations in the country, was returned in a huge 7.7 per cent swing. Emerging triumphant onto the steps of Birmingham Town Hall after the count, he declared:

We have buried the race issue.

This analysis was, as things turned out, a trifle optimistic, but the results throughout the country showed that, for the moment at any rate, Smethwick was a name for the history books and that the immigration bandwagon had ground to a temporary halt. 'It looks at long last,' trumpeted the *Guardian* editorial (24 May), 'as though the long winter of Smethwick and Leyton is nearing an end.'

As the issue lost its potential as a vote-winner, so Enoch Powell lost public interest in it.

During the election campaign, Powell had concentrated on other issues. On 16 March, at Darlington, he had described the Government's foreign policy as 'an indistinguishable echo of the State Department'. On Saturday 26 March, he travelled to Falkirk in Scotland where, in front of television cameras which happened by some miracle to be in Falkirk at the time, Powell attempted to 'transform' the Conservative campaign with a remarkable revelation. He would not be surprised, he said, if the Ministry of Defence did not have contingency plans for sending British troops to Vietnam. 'It would be intolerable,' he said, 'if this was to happen, and the Prime Minister ought to confirm or deny it now.'

This intervention at a crucial stage in the election campaign tells us a lot about Enoch Powell and his methods in opposition. There was for the suggestion that the Labour Government would send troops to Vietnam not a scintilla of evidence. Nor did Powell supply any evidence. He repeated a reckless rumour, and, by doing so earnestly in front of the television cameras, made the rumour respectable and almost credible. The speech ran contrary to Conservative Party policy and Conservative Party tactics. In the war in Vietnam, the British Conservative Party stood 'one hundred per cent behind our American allies'. The anti-Americanism of Powell's speeches and their suggestion that a Conservative Government would not send troops to fight communists in the Far East if asked to do so by allies, was bitterly resented by traditional Tories throughout the country. The wretched Edward Heath, leading his Party to its biggest peacetime defeat at the polls since 1906, had a further problem to contend with. At the Conservative Party Press Conference the following day Heath described his Shadow Minister of Defence's allegations as 'a strictly personal expression of opinion for which the Conservative Party has no responsibility'. (*Daily Telegraph*, 28 March 1966). Under a barrage of questions about Powell's speech, Heath writhed uncomfortably, admitting that it was 'possible' that Powell, as Shadow Minister of Defence, had some information which could give the allegations substance. In the meantime, the Defence Minister, Mr Denis Healey, and the Prime Minsiter were jubilantly denying the allegations, adding that Powell had refused to attend briefings at the Ministry of Defence, and therefore had no inside information. The firework which Powell had planted was quickly doused.

Powell greeted his Party's defeat at the polls with something approaching jubilation. All the responsibilities of office were now swept aside for a long period. A week after the results were declared, he delivered an ecstatic call to arms to the City of London Young Conservatives:

The levers of power have been removed from our reach, or even our remote control. . . . 'Words not action' describes with precision the role of the Conservative Party as this new phase opens in its and the nation's political life . . . some of our words will be harsh, fierce, destructive words, aimed in defiance and contempt at men and policies we detest. . . . Of course they will be negative, combative, nay-saying words, designed to demolish, to shake confidence, to hold up to ridicule. . . . We have liberty to question and to propose without fearing the jealous scrutiny for pedantic consistency to which the words of a party in office or on the brink of it are forever of necessity obnoxious. (*The Times*, 7 April 1966).

All this was quite contrary to the strategy of the Tory leadership, which clung still to the principles of their election manifesto 'Action, not Words', which Powell had mischievously turned upside down. What Edward Heath wanted was, not a return to ideological argument or a theoretical 're-think', but, as *The Times* Political correspondent put it (4 April) 'a clear, cohesive commitment to a set of policies . . . that it would carry into action as a Government'.

Heath's fury at this overt challenge to his strategy was compounded into blind rage when, on 10 April, with Heath out of the country, Powell blithely issued a Press statement on the Government's blockade of Beira to prevent oil reaching Rhodesia. No subject was more sensitive to the Tory leadership than Rhodesian sanctions, yet Powell made his undisguised attack on oil sanctions without first consulting Reginald Maudling, acting Tory leader in Heath's absence.

On Friday 15 April, Powell was summoned to Heath's flat in the Albany, and told bluntly that if we wished to stay in the Shadow Cabinet he would have to stop making public statements which were contrary to Party policy. The result of the meeting was described by the *Sunday Times* (17 April) as

a notable achievement for Mr Heath. It means he can launch his reconstructed Shadow Cabinet team this week without the fear that Mr Powell's dissident voice might exert a counter-pull on Tory loyalties from the backbenches.

'Wherever he (Powell) goes', was the *Sunday Times*'s prediction,

he will accept the general Shadow Cabinet Rule – that he issues statements only on his specific responsibility, and then generally after consultation with the Leader, and that any speeches he makes on other matters will be by arrangement with the colleague most concerned.

For a time, it looked as though a genuine truce had been agreed. Powell told the Wembley Young Conservatives:

I'm very satisfied to be led and very happy to serve with and under Mr Heath. (*Guardian*, 10 May 1966).

In June, Heath travelled to Washington and was asked at a Press Conference:

Is Mr Powell under wraps and will he stay there?

To which he replied:

Yes to both questions – at least he was when I left, and I think he has talked about nothing since but milk and the Co-ops. (*Daily Express*, 4 June 1966).

No reply could have been more calculated to infuriate Powell, who had indeed, until then, observed relative silence. It may well have been Heath's cocky quip in Washington which drove Powell onto the offensive once again. He embarked at once on a series of controversial speeches, attacking such Gods of the Heath technocracy as 'the nonsense' of productivity (30 September) and distinguished company chairmen who played ball with the Government, notably by responding to the calls of the Bank of England for information about overseas investments. (5 November).

There was, however, one subject to which Mr Powell did not return during 1966: immigration. This was a period in which the 'liberal view' on immigration continued to dominate the thinking of all parties. The Home Secretary, Roy Jenkins, was converting traditional Home Office restrictionism into an interest in race relations. In his speech to the National Committee of Commonwealth Immigrants on 23 May, he hinted that he was not opposed to extending the existing, almost worthless Race Relations Act into the fields of housing and employment. His attitude to race relations delighted race relations workers and liberals who today, in some disillusionment, look back to the period as a Golden Era.

During the eighteen months following the 1966 election, when the numbers of Commonwealth immigrants entering the country continued at a rate of more than 50,000 a year, Powell made no speeches demanding further immigration control. Those who did continue with such demands were isolated and rejected as never before. In the debate on the Expiring Laws Continuance Bill in November 1966, Cyril Osborne and Harold Gurden went through the ritual motions of demanding more controls and were joined this time by Duncan Sandys whose fits of pique since being removed from the Shadow Cabinet in 1965 were a standard political joke. Such demands received no publicity and even less support. Meanwhile, the local 'community relations' committees established by the 'integrative proposals' in the August 1965 White Paper started to get down to work, and their effect, combined with the mild political temperature and a liberal Home Secretary, produced evidence of a distinct improvement in British race relations.

In the early months of 1967, Powell threw all caution to the winds in an attempt to raise the political temperature on a variety of issues, almost all of which were delicate subjects for the Conservative leadership. On 11 January in Birmingham, he ridiculed Government attempts to persuade industry to export more, specifically referring to Mr Harold Macmillan's famous phrase 'exporting is fun'. This speech did not commend itself to Mr Edward Heath, founder of the British National Export Council. In the same speech, Powell advocated a floating exchange rate for sterling which was not part of Conservative official policy. The next day, in Wolverhampton, Powell said that trade unions as such were 'harmful to the country at large' and the day after, in Birmingham again, he attacked political 'interference' in the 'housing market', blaming 'political parties' in general. In the first three months of 1967, he launched a savage attack on the Government's prices and incomes legislation, openly waged war with Reginald Maudling, the Conservatives' deputy leader, on whether or not a prices and incomes policy was possible in principle, and could claim much of the credit for pushing the Tories into outright opposition to the prices and incomes legislation. (Powell was a member of the Cabinet when the first Prices and Incomes Board, then called the National Incomes Commission, and his other bugbear, the National Economic Development Council, were first established.) He had warned a

Scottish Young Unionist rally at Peebles not to treat the National Incomes Commission as a joke, and the Government's 'pay pause' of 1961 as a thing of the past.

'The validity of the policy,' he said,

is unchallenged and unchallengeable. Its realization required the abandonment of habits and thought and behaviour ingrained from past generations which knew nothing of the State's unlimited power to create new money . . . (*Sunday Times*, 11 November 1962).

Few Conservative Cabinet Ministers at the time were prepared to go so far in expounding classical Keynesianism.

In the first seven weeks of 1967, Powell delivered twenty-six speeches, sixteen of them in public, ten of them in private. All of them were carefully prepared. Many of them were issued to the Press before delivery. None of them caused any pleasure in the Albany flat of Mr Edward Heath, and few of the more controversial ones had been cleared with him before delivery. Powell's speech on incomes policy in March was, according to the *Observer* (19 March 1967), 'not cleared with Heath'. The Lord President of the Council, Mr Richard Crossman, rubbed salt in the wounds of the Tory leadership, by asking in Coventry:

What is happening inside the Tory leadership? Who is running the Opposition? Certainly not the titular leader who sits nervously strumming on his piano in Albany while our latter-day Savonarola rampages round the country summoning devout congregations of the faithful to reject as heretics those Conservative leaders all of whom, in his view, have departed from the straight and narrow path of 19th century *laissez faire*' (*The Times*, 16 January 1967).

This was plausible propaganda, but it bore little relation to the real situation. True, Enoch Powell was a permanent irritant to Edward Heath. But there was at that time no sign that, in spite of all his efforts, he was making any substantial impact on national politics, or on the balance of power in the Conservative Party. Edward Heath still drooped in the opinion polls, but none of his obvious rivals – Maudling, Macleod, Hogg, Home – were doing any better, and Powell was hardly mentioned. It is true that Powell commanded bigger audiences than most other Tory leaders; true too that he was greatly respected in the constituencies for the rigour of his thinking and his simplistic approach to the economic problems of modern monopoly capitalism. But in the spring of 1967, in spite of all these speeches, Enoch Powell was still regarded more as a 'bit of a character' and 'a maverick' than a serious contender for the Party leadership. Similarly his speeches were not striking the spark which, he hoped, would ignite the popular imagination.

During those months, Enoch Powell referred only once to immigration: in a long, leader-page review of a book about Sparkbrook, Birmingham, in the *Daily Telegraph*. Some of this review has been quoted elsewhere (see page 62), but there is one passage in it which refers directly to Powell's views at the time:

For the moment, compared with the past decade or so, there is a feeling of stabilization; the immigrants are 'shaking down' and 'shaking out' rather than visibly increasing; and the subject has disappeared below the surface of public consciousness. In my own constituency ... I have the impression that, as no doubt elsewhere, the first phase, the sudden impact of Commonwealth immigration is over.

I am going to prophesy, however, that there will be subsequent phases, when the problem will resume its place in public concern and in a more intractable form, when it can no longer be dealt with simply by turning the inlet tap down or off.

The reason for this prophecy is not entire clear from Mr Powell's article. There is no explanation as to why the 'stabilization' then achieved should disintegrate. But the failure to explain the reasons for his prophecy did not deflect from Mr Powell's confidence as to its accuracy. The most successful prophet is one who knows that, if all else fails, he himself will be able to ensure the fulfilment of his own predictions.

For the moment, however, there was 'a feeling of stabilization' and therefore little chance of any response to a campaign. This 'feeling of stablization', however, was not, as Powell would have it, because 'the first impact of immigration is over', but as a result of the swing of the political pendulum away from a preoccupation with controls towards 'integration'. This process was epitomized in April 1967 by the change of mind of the country's two biggest trade unions about the need to make racial discrimination in employment illegal.

Accordingly, in June, the Home Secretary announced his intention of bringing in a new Race Relations Bill which would make discrimination in housing and employment illegal.

The liberals' Golden Hour in British race relations was, however, drawing to a close. Imperceptibly at first, then with rapidly gathering speed the immigration control bandwagon started to roll again. A series of articles in journals like the *News of the World, Tit-Bits,* and *Reveille* during the spring and early summer marked the change of mood. Race riots in America, particularly in Detroit, added fuel to the flames. On 9 July Enoch Powell wrote an article in the *Sunday Express* headed 'CAN WE AFFORD TO LET OUR RACE PROBLEM EXPLODE?' in which he argued, for the first time specifically, that the families of immigrants already here should be kept out. By now he could explain his escape from his inescapable obligation of humanity with a piece of facile facetiousness.

When the consequences of an unrestricted right of entry for dependants are so grave, it is reasonable to point out that families can also be reunited by immigrants returning home.

This line was taken up by Duncan Sandys in a highly publicized speech on 24 July, in which he also called for a ban on dependants. Attacking a recent Government publication 'Immigrants and the Youth Service', which asked its readers to accept mixed marriages, Sandys declared, charitably:

The breeding of millions of half-caste children would merely produce a generation of misfits and create national tensions.

This line was taken up with vigour after the summer holidays. On 4 September, a letter appeared in the *Daily Telegraph* from Mr Tom Iremonger, telling its readers of 'indisputable evidence of a racialist campaign to infiltrate local Tory organizations'. On 13 September the Monday Club called a big meeting in Caxton Hall to pass a motion, moved by Cyril Osborne, for 'stringent limitation of immigration into the United Kingdom for the next five years'. The 'good-natured, friendly English people,' said the good-natured, friendly, Sir Cyril, 'have started to commit race suicide.' (*Nottingham Guardian Journal*, 14 September 1967).

On 20 September Duncan Sandys made another highly publicized speech calling for 'turning off the tap', and achieved more publicity through a dispute with the Lambeth Council for Community Relations. On 25 September a coloured Conservative candidate for the Hornsey borough council elections resigned because of the increasing influence of racialism in the Party.

For a moment, opinion in the Conservative Party seemed to hang in the balance. On 28 September Edward Heath spoke to a women's meeting in Ipswich 'in what' according to the political correspondent of the *Western Mail*, 'was seen as a rebuff to the anti-immigrant lobby in his Party'. He advocated continuing strict control, voluntary repatriation measures, but, above all, the acceptance of all immigrants on an equal basis. 'Race relations,' he said, 'should not become a Party issue.' The attitude of Conservative Central Office was outlined by Mr Ben Patterson, research assistant to the Conservative Political Centre, who assured Wolverhampton Young Conservatives that 'piecemeal efforts would at least eventually create a position of mutual tolerance'. (*Express and Star*, 20 September 1967).

Enoch Powell, still a member of the Shadow Cabinet, had not yet decided to throw himself wholeheartedly into an anti-immigration campaign. Apart from two articles, he had not made any major statement on the subject since the general election eighteen months earlier. On 7 October he addressed a large meeting at Gloucester on the helplessness of the individual before Government bureaucracy. Immigration was not mentioned in the speech, but it arose at question time, and Powell did not disappoint the audience with his replies. The *Gloucester Citizen*, which never loses an opportunity to give publicity to the case against immigration, used these replies as their front-page lead in their issue of 9 October under a banner headline: 'POWELL DEMANDS IMMIGRATION CURBS.'

'Limiting immigration to Britain,' said Powell,

is an understatement of what is required and is no less than our duty to future generations of this country. . . . We not only have to secure no addition to the Commonwealth immigrants still coming at an annual intake of 50,000, but we have got to establish an outgoing for those not fitting in, or fitting in less well, in what is called, in sociologists' jargon, 'the host country'. They must return to the country where they belong.

The British people have been told that they must deny that there is any difference between those who belong to this country and 'those others'. If you persist in asserting what is an undeniable truth, you will be hounded and pilloried as a racialist.

Exactly three years previously, in a special election article, Powell had written:

I will always set my face like flint against making any difference between one citizen of this country and another on grounds of his origin.

Now he was proclaiming these differences as 'an undeniable truth'. The deterioration in his attitude marked the difference between Enoch Powell in October 1964, dipping his toe gingerly into the waters of immigration controversy, and shielding himself from criticism with high-flown phrases about racial equality, and Enoch Powell in October 1967 splashing about recklessly, abandoning former phrases about racial equality, for further demands for restriction and further emphasis on the differences between the immigrant and 'the host'.

There was, moreover, a new issue which gave specific impetus to the general demands for immigration control: the immigration of Asians from Kenya. This immigration dated back to the Kenyan Independence Act of 1963, by which, after protracted constitutional talks, the Conservative Government granted independence to Kenya. The Government at the time, and the Commonwealth Secretary of State, Mr Duncan Sandys, were concerned above all to protect the white settlers of Kenya from future embarrassment at the hands of the African Government. They therefore included in the Bill a clause giving the right to citizens in Kenya to hold on to their British citizenship rather than become citizens of the new Kenya. There was to be a two year 'period of grace' during which such citizens would be able to choose whether they wanted to remain as citizens of the United Kingdom or become citizens of Kenya.

This special clause was designed solely as an escape hatch for the Kenya whites. But it was complicated by the position of the Asians in Kenya, most of whom were merchants and who, as a community, had played an ambiguous role in the Kenyan Africans' long struggle for independence. The question, which was never openly resolved, was:

Did the British Government intend that Kenyans could hold onto British citizenship, with all the rights of that citizenship, including the right of free entry to Britain?

Asked specifically about this in the House of Commons, Sandys prevaricated:

'I would think,' he said,

once they have acquired a Commonwealth citizenship and have given up their United Kingdom citizenship, they would be treated as citizens of the Commonwealth country of which they belong ... but they may for a period still have United Kingdom citizenship before they opt for Commonwealth citizenship. (Hansard, 28 November 1963).

The question, however, was whether they would be allowed to hold onto United Kingdom citizenship after the two-year period, and therefore would have the right to enter Britain. There was no specific pledge, but the Kenyan Asian community was left in little doubt that they would indeed be allowed, like the Europeans, to hold onto United Kingdom citizenship, and therefore come into the country free of the controls of the Commonwealth Immigrants Act, 1962. In an article in the *Spectator*, in February 1968, Mr Iain Macleod, who was Minister of Labour at the time of the Kenyan Independence Act, argued that the Conservative Government had deliberately extended the right of free entry to the Kenyan Asians. 'We did it,' he wrote. 'We meant to do it, and in any case we had no other alternative.'

In an unshown television interview, quoted in David Steel's *No Entry* (Hurst, 1969, p. 63), Mr Tom Mboya, who was Minister of Justice following independence, said:

We would only have one citizenship – and Britain decided in the circumstances that they would make it possible for certain categories of people, not only Asians, to retain British citizenship.

As a result of Mr Sandys's legislation, some 100,000 Kenyan Asians clung to their British citizenship until after the interregnum expired in 1965. There was no warning from either Conservative or Labour Governments that this citizenship would not bring with it a right of free entry to Britain and throughout the four years 1964–8 Kenyan Asians entered Britain free of control. In 1966, and especially in 1967, however, the Kenyan Government stepped up its programme of 'Africanization' with the result that more Kenyan Asians started to enter the country. This situation led Mr Duncan Sandys, under whose legislation the right of free entry had been granted to Kenyan Asians, to start a popular campaign to break the obligations which he had entered into.

The first major speech calling for controls of the Kenyan Asians was made by Enoch Powell. In characteristic mischief, Powell chose to make a major speech on the subject during the Conservative Party Conference, which he ignored.

'When Kenya became independent in 1963,' he told a Conservative meeting at Deal in Kent,

Parliament enacted that anybody who then became a citizen of Kenya automatically ceased to be a citizen of the United Kingdom and colonies. It was, however, Kenya who defined their own citizens and they did so in such a way as to exclude hundreds of thousands of Asiatics and others who were residing there.

These people, explained Powell, now had a right of free entry into the country because they were citizens of the United Kingdom and colonies.

By a decision of the Kenya legislature, defining a Kenya citizen, hundreds of thousands of people in Kenya who had not belonged to this country before and never dreamt that they did started to belong to it just like you and me. . . . It is quite monstrous that an unforeseen loophole in legislation should be able to add another quarter of a million to that score without any control or limit whatever.

The Kenya legislature had, in fact, denied no one who was living in Kenya at the time of independence citizenship of Kenya. They had merely made it clear that they would not tolerate dual citizenship (a concept which Powell has often ridiculed). The British Tory Government in 1963, with Powell in its cabinet, had offered an option of maintaining British citizenship to certain minorities in Kenya, including the Asians. The Asians who took out this option, and clung on to their British citizenship were not allowed to become Kenyan citizens as well. This situation was due, not to 'a decision of the Kenya legislature', which did not define citizenship on racial lines, but to a decision of the British Government of which Powell was a member. The 'unforeseeable loophole' had been created by a British Conservative Government which, at the time of handing over one of the last and most prized possessions of its Empire, still felt some obligation to the minorities in that Empire who had in the past stood by the British against the 'native' majority. When, as a result of those obligations, brown faces appeared at London airport, decent Conservative gentlemen like Powell and Sandys started to describe their own previous decisions as 'unforeseeable loopholes'.

Powell's speech at Deal, as no doubt he had calculated, got rather more publicity than the deliberations of the Conservative Party in conference at Scarborough. (Powell once described party conferences as 'jamborees, festivals, games, not serious gatherings. They are a nuisance':) In the *Daily Express* the following day (19 October), Wilfrid Sendall sensed further irritation in the Tory leadership.

Mr Edward Heath and his colleagues are alarmed at the possible charge that they would like to discriminate on purely racial grounds in favour of Europeans as against Asiatics.

This was a deliberately-inspired leak from the Tory leadership, and was printed in almost exactly the same form in a number of local papers (notably the *Wolverhampton Express and Star*). The Tory leadership at that time, and for some weeks afterwards, was more than a little embarrassed by the campaign to keep out the Kenyan Asians. When Sandys raised the matter in the Expiring Laws Continuance Bill debate on 15 November, he was firmly slapped down by the Home Secretary, Roy Jenkins, and the Conservative frontbench remained uneasily silent. Heath had spoken three days earlier in Plymouth, and, in reply to questions on immigration, he had underlined the need for strict control of immigration because of the need to treat people equally once they were here.

Enoch Powell, however, was discovering that the response to these speeches and answers on immigration was very much greater than the response to his speeches on any other single subject. On 19 November he spoke in Bournemouth to 800 Bournemouth, Christchurch and Poole Tories, packed into the Pavilion. Once again, immigration arose at question time, and once again this was the subject singled out by the local paper for special treatment.

'Immigrants to this country at the rate of 50,000 a year,' said Powell,

would reach half a million in ten years. This is approximately the American proportion. Coloured labour by the end of the century would be a serious problem...

The Conservative policy is that the inflow of immigrants should be greatly reduced. Dependants should count for whatever total number it was thought should be allowed in year by year. Assistance should also be given to voluntary repatriation of immigrants. (*Bournemouth Evening Echo*, 20 November 1967).

All this was very well received, as was the helpful rejoinder from the local M.P., Mr John Cordle, who spoke with all the love for humanity of a director of a Church of England newspaper:

In thirty years we could be a coffee-coloured nation.

As the response to such statements increased in volume and enthusiasm, so did Enoch Powell's statements about immigration. On 9 December, at a meeting of his local constituency, he denounced 'the folly' of Commonwealth immigration and again predicted 500,000 more immigrants in ten years. Together with Sandys, Osborne and other Conservative M.P.s, he had succeeded in keeping immigration in the headlines for three months. In the country at large, despite the publication of the Street Report in November and other measures and recommendations for integration, public opinion was responding readily to the Sandys/Powell/Osborne initiative. Writing in *The Times* of 5 December, Professor T. F. Pettigrew, a social psychologist from Harvard, took the view that 'race relations in Britain are deteriorating rapidly'.

For a few brief weeks, over Christmas and the New Year, public controversy on immigration was suspended. Enoch Powell managed to avoid mentioning immigration during January, though he infuriated his leader once more with a speech at Wolverhampton in which he savaged the Backing Britain movement as 'ineffably silly and positively dangerous'. The Backing Britain fiasco had been started at a Surrey firm of heating engineers, whose managing director was a personal friend of a Conservative frontbencher, Mr John Boyd Carpenter. Mr Heath, moreover, had jumped very swiftly onto the Back Britain bandwagon and had sent a telegram of congratulation to the firm. 'He has,' said the *Daily Telegraph* political correspondent (on 11 January) 'admired the spirit of the Surrey typists, and must be annoyed with Mr Powell for his outright condemnation'.

There was however no time to dally with such minor irritants. Powell's speech attacking the Backing Britain movement resulted in little publicity and even less support. It was time to return to immigration and this Powell did in no uncertain terms at a Conservative dinner at Walsall, on 9 February.

The speech dealt in the main with figures for immigration, arguing that the rate of immigration was still far too high. The respect which Mr Powell shows for statistics when the right ones do not fit his case was ably demonstrated by the lynchpin of his argument in this speech:

If we continue to admit by voucher about 8,000 male immigrants a year with an unrestricted right of entry for dependants, the present inflow... will be easily maintained.

The total number of male voucher-holders entering Britain in 1966 was 4,365: in 1967 it was 3,807. Powell's figure was double the real one.

'It follows,' argued Powell triumphantly from these false statistical premises, that either the issue of vouchers must be virtually terminated, or the unconditional right of entry for dependants withdrawn, or both.

Finally, Powell turned his attention to the Kenyan Asians. '200,000 Indians in Kenya alone,' he said, 'have an absolute right of entry to this country.' This was very surprising since the Kenya Statistical Digest of 1967 estimated the Asian population as 192,000 of whom some 70,000 had chosen to become citizens of Kenya (and were thus subject to British immigration controls). Many more were citizens of India or Pakistan; others were British subjects without citizenship. Mr Powell once again had arrived at a figure which was approximately double the real one.

Despite such flaws, the speech received a great deal of publicity all over the country. The *Sunday Express* and the *Daily Sketch* devoted editorials to praising Powell. For the next few days, Powell, Sandys and their anti-immigration lobby devoted all their powers to maintaining the pressure on the issue of the Kenyan Asians. On 11 February, two days after Powell's speech, Sandys said that the situation was 'getting out of hand' and called for 'drastic legislation to curb the flow of dependants from the Commonwealth and of Kenyan Asians in general'. On 12 February, Powell said on the BBC programme, Panorama, 'We ought to have power over dependants.' Asked whether this was contrary to Conservative Party policy, he replied 'certainly not, certainly not', despite repeated assurances from Conservative Party leaders that the families of immigrants already here should be allowed in free of control.

Powell was also asked about the Kenyan Asians and curiously did not even have the courage to demand that these be controlled. He complained that the Government had been 'absolutely inactive' on the problem (the Government in fact had been desperately seeking some way of keeping the Kenyan Asians out without legislation). Pressed twice by Robin Day to state whether he favoured restriction of the Kenyan Asians, Powell refused to commit himself.

Ten days hard campaigning later, the Government collapsed, and announced plans to introduce a voucher system controlling the immigration of Kenyan Asians. Smartly, the

Opposition stepped into line. The Bill was rushed through Parliament in a day and a night (29 February / 1 March) with the support of Mr Duncan Sandys and Mr Enoch Powell, who was the politician most responsible for changing the Government's (and the Opposition's) mind. All this brought Powell a flood of publicity and correspondence. The enthusiasm for his views on immigration quite startled him. He had never realized before what combustible material the immigration issue was.

As for his relations with the Shadow Cabinet, they had grown, if possible, even worse. Two days after the Walsall speech, Heath had told the Young Conservatives Conference at Harrogate: 'Of course, Mr Powell has nothing to do with racialism either. Let's be quite clear about that.' (*Sun*, 12 February 1968). In the privacy of the Shadow Cabinet, however, Powell was rebuked by Iain Macleod for the tone and language of his Walsall speech. When Powell, objecting, started to refer to his speech, Heath interrupted begging him not to go through it all again. Powell's protestations that he had no idea that the Shadow Cabinet would disapprove of his later speeches were, in the light of this reaction, a trifle disingenuous.

But outside the Shadow Cabinet and outside Parliament, where Powell preferred not to engage in the immigration debate, things were different. One of the most constant rules in the history of immigration control is that those demanding controls are encouraged, not silenced, by concessions. The Commonwealth Immigrants Act, 1968, far from stemming the tide, encouraged it still further. After a lull of a fortnight, the bandwagon sped on. On 28 February, Councillor Franklin, Tory chairman of Birmingham Corporation's Health Committee, issued a Press statement about immigrant pressure on hospital and maternity services. The Press crawled with stories of racial conflict: busmen in Wolverhampton complaining about a Corporation ban on turbans; the acquittal of four men charged with incitement to racial hatred by the circulation of Racial Preservation Society documents and, on 8 April, the publication of the Race Relations Bill. On that day, Duncan Sandys issued a statement calling for a complete cessation of immigration 'for several years' to help make the Bill work. Immigrants, he said, 'must make a greater effort to conform to British standards and the British way of life'. (*Guardian*, 9 April 1968).

Yet still it seemed unlikely that the anti-immigration lobby would break through the political sound barrier. Sandys himself, for all his experience as an ex-Minister, had made no more than a dent in the apparently invulnerable edifice of the consensus, and the rest of the anti-immigration lobby in the Conservative Parliamentary lobby – Osborne, Bell, Gurden – were of no real political significance. Enoch Powell was not rated in the opinion polls' Conservative leaders' charts. Calling simply for more immigration controls was established practice which was unlikely seriously to disturb either Front Bench in Parliament or to mobilize the masses outside. The game, up to and even including the Walsall speech, had, as it were, been played according to the rules of normal political controversy. What was required was a new tone, a new dimension. It was this problem which worried Enoch Powell as he pondered over the hundreds of enthusiastic letters which responded to his Walsall speech. The result was his speech at Birmingham on 20 April which resulted in his being sacked from the Shadow Cabinet and achieving a higher rating in the polls than the leader who sacked him. The business of setting light to what he had once called 'combustible material' was triumphantly completed in the Birmingham speech.

The qualitative difference between Powell's Birmingham speech and the speeches on immigration which he and other respectable Conservative leaders had made in the past was not so much in the warnings of blood to come, as in the recitation of statements and stories from correspondents. Before his Birmingham speech, Powell had acquired a partially-deserved reputation for intellectual independence. He had argued that the task of a modern politician was not to mouth the politics of his constituents (which is impossible, since such politics are never homogenous), but to arrive at conclusions by thinking problems through. Thus, as recently as January 1968, Enoch Powell, alone of all leading politicians in the country, had refused to bow at the altar of the Backing

Britain movement. By contrast, at Birmingham in April, he quoted an anonymous constituent of his saying that 'in this country in fifteen or twenty years time, the black man will have the whiphand over the white man'.

This was meaningless and pernicious nonsense. But Powell justified his repeating such a remark, and sympathizing with it. 'I do not,' he said,

have the right not to do so. Here is a decent, ordinary fellow-Englishman who in broad daylight in my own town says to me, his Member of Parliament, that this country will not be worth living in for his children. I simply do not have the right to shrug my shoulders and think of something else.

Let us suppose for a moment that an ordinary decent fellow-Englishman were to approach Powell in the streets of Wolverhampton and suggest to him that the capitalist system was so intolerable that Britain in a few years time would not be worth living in. Would Powell feel duty bound to retail that message to his next meeting? If hundreds of thousands of people argued the same thing, would Powell feel even more obliged to fall into line? The truth is that Powell would reject the man's complaint, because he disagrees with it. Popularly-held views do not have to be accepted by politicians just because they are popularly-held. This excuse, used so expertly by Peter Griffiths at Smethwick in 1964, for failing properly to argue a point of view – that it is the view of constituents – is an evasion of those political responsibilities of which Enoch Powell was once a champion.

In matters of race relations, it is even worse. In the decade before Powell's Birmingham speech, race relations had been bedevilled by a vocal underworld of gossip-mongers, spreading stories about the bad behaviour of coloured immigrants.

The anecdotes followed a pattern. In 1964–5 I travelled round the country's immigrant areas talking to people who held strongly anti-immigrant views. In Southall, Birmingham and Bradford, I was told that 'an old lady of sixty-eight' had been accosted by a coloured man. (In one case she had been raped.) Other familiar themes were the carefree scattering of excrement by immigrants, their endless quest for sex, the smell of their food, the noise of West Indian parties, the harassment of old ladies by landlords and potential house-buyers, and, perhaps most scurrilous of all, the use of children as propagandists of race hatred. Common to all examples are their anonymity. As Mrs Ann Dummett, an Oxford voluntary race relations worker, wrote to *The Times* soon after Powell's Birmingham speech:

A large number of racialist anecdotes are in circulation. Every attempt I have made, when told such stories, to find evidence for them has failed. Nobody ever knows the names and addresses of the people involved. (24 April 1968).

These fables often stem from genuine irritation about food smells or party noises, but are exploited by racialists into horror stories. The literature of the extreme right throughout the 1960s reeks of this mythology. The August–October 1961 issue of *Combat,* organ of the British National Party, for instance, retails a story of a white lady coming back from work one night, pursued as ever by sex-crazed Indians. Looking up, she even saw a naked immigrant in a tree!

'I know a married woman,' recounts a correspondent,

pushing a baby in its pram, who was stopped five times in less than a mile by a coloured man. (*Combat*, Sept./Oct. 1963).

The British National Party had a strong base in Southall, and some close friends in the Southall Residents Association which soon degenerated into an anti-immigration organization. Reporting an SRA meeting in its January/March issue of 1964, *Combat* announced:

Some elderly women were nearly in tears as they revealed how Indians were blocking drains with stagnant refuse, threatening them when they protested, urinating and excreting in the streets, living in garden sheds, entertaining prostitutes, accosting local white women, fighting among themselves and with West Indians – and of their methods in driving out sitting white tenants.

This last point was later developed in a 'survey' of coloured immigration by Colin Jordan's National Socialist Movement:

In their efforts to evict white tenants so that they can replace them with coloured people, coloured landlords and tenants resort to every kind of nuisance and intimidation. Deliberate, continual noise at all hours, systematic insults, threats and violence and actual assaults, calculated humiliation and obscenities are among the methods employed.

Among the mass of evidence that has been put before us by white victims of these methods, we have for instance photographs showing human excreta deposited by blacks outside the door of a white woman's flat in London as part of their campaign to get rid of her. (*Nat. Socialist* April/June 1965.)

And in the same month, Mr Dennis Pirie, a BNP leader, declared:

I can attest to cases where pensioners have been to M.P.s of both parties for protection from their black gangster landlords. (*Combat*, April 1965).

These stories, and many like them, must have come to the ears of any M.P. or councillor for an immigrant area. It must have been this kind of story which Powell heard from the delegation from the Wolverhampton branch of the British Immigration Control Association which visited him in 1961. Yet the unanimous reaction of M.P.s up to that time was to refer the story-teller to a local official, and publicly to ignore it – partly because in most cases the facts could not be proved, and partly because, even in the few cases where they could be proved, the simple recitation of these facts in public would give the entirely false impression that such behaviour was typical of the immigrant community.

It was this tradition which Powell broke on 20 April in Birmingham. In his speech he retailed a story which, he said, came from a correspondent in Northumberland. (This alone was enough to raise a hearty laugh from race relations workers, who have noticed that the further away from immigrants the origin of the reports, the more fantastic they become.) The story was about a white old lady in a Wolverhampton street surrounded by immigrants, who was persecuted and pestered by her coloured neighbours. First, her windows are broken, then, inevitably, 'she finds excreta pushed through her letter-box'. She is abused as a 'racialist' by 'charming, wide-eyed, grinning piccaninnies'. And so on.

No one, despite endless inquiries and research, could find

any trace of such a lady in Wolverhampton. Even Powell had not said that she existed. He had merely said that a correspondent in Northumberland had *said* that she existed. He admitted some months later (on January 3 1969) on the Frost Programme that he had not checked whether or not the old lady existed, and did not know whether she existed or not. While politicians of all parties in the past had hesitated to give publicity to proved cases of bad immigrant behaviour for fear of smearing all immigrants with an unrepresentative example, Powell had given the most extensive publicity possible to a case which was wholly unproved and almost certainly apocryphal.[1]

The same stories and the same language before 20 April 1968, had been used almost exclusively by extremists and racialists, and had been greeted with widespread cynicism. After 20 April 1968 the ugliest fears of people who knew nothing of immigration problems were confirmed. Those who sought scapegoats had found a champion. Powell's speech and his instantaneous dismissal from the Shadow Cabinet earned him what he had sought after for so long: extensive publicity for his every speech and statement. The cuttings libraries of the national newspapers had to open new folders for Powell. The mass media from all over the world rushed to comment on this new phenomenon in British politics. Meat

[1] According to The Milner Holland Report on London Housing (1965. Cmnd. 2605), which Powell, also on the Frost Programme, claimed as evidence for his stories about coloured landlords.

'If the position were to be assessed only by the more sensational stories current during the height of the public outcry about the landlord persecutions, or even by the individual cases brought to our notice, it would be natural to reach a facile conclusion that the prime offender was a coloured landlord. The general impression is in part undoubtedly due to an ingrained fear and apprehension, whether rational or irrational, inspired by the coloured landlord, who is differentiated not only by his appearance, but also by habits, ways of life and, in some sections, language difficulties as well. In the result, a bad coloured landlord tends to give a bad name to all of his kind – a striking instance of the tendency to generalize from the particular. We have tried to test the validity of this general impression ... and ... we have no reason to believe that there is an exceptionally high incidence of abuses in property for which coloured landlords are responsible. (pp. 190, 191.)

porters from Smithfield, led by a supporter of Sir Oswald Mosley, and dockers from Tilbury marched to Parliament in support of Powell – though a dockers' one-day strike and march the following week attracted only a small minority. Mr Jenkins, Chancellor of the Exchequer (on 4 May) and the Prime Minister (on 5 May) made speeches attacking Powell, while Mr Heath's prompt action in dismissing Powell was, in the immediate period following Powell's speech, well received in the official Conservative leadership. But soon the anti-immigration lobby in the Party began to move under the new impetus which Powell's speech had given it. Parliamentary revolts broke out in the summer against the leadership over their moderate approach to the Race Relations Bill, and the Party's spokesman for Home Affairs, Mr Quintin Hogg, was heckled from his backbenches as he summed up for the Opposition on the Bill's third reading. On 20 September, the Conservative Party Conference agenda was published, showing eighty resolutions on immigration, four times as many as the previous year when the Kenyan Asians had been uncontrolled. The great majority of the resolutions were to the right of Party policy, which itself was moved substantially further to the right by the Party leader, Edward Heath, who spoke on immigration at York on the day of the agenda's publication. Heath's speech for the first time committed the Conservatives to applying the same laws to Commonwealth immigrants as to aliens – a process whose main affect would be to deny Commonwealth immigrants the rights of citizenship on entering the country. Citizenship would be obtained, said Heath, 'not, as at present as of right, but only by immigrants of good character'. The speech also committed the Party to control – 'on humanitarian grounds' which were not specified – of dependants.

The speech was almost wholly negative, obsessed with controls, and marked a decisive shift towards the demands of Enoch Powell. But Powell was not to be outflanked. If his demands for tighter immigration control were met, he would simply demand more. In a brief intervention at the Conservative Party Conference (the speech was handed out to the Press beforehand and recited word for word), Powell did just that:

I want to say one thing only to this conference: we deceive ourselves if we imagine, whatever steps are taken to limit further immigration, that this country will still not be facing a prospect which is unacceptable.

In other words, it was no longer enough to talk of immigration solely in terms of control. An even more important demand was that of 'assisted repatriation and resettlement'. It was not merely a question of keeping the blacks out; it was a question of sending them home. Powell was arguing that repatriation, which until that time had been an unimportant addendum to official Conservative policy, must now become a central issue. This further move to the Right brought a third of the conference cheering to their feet, and evoked from Mr Quintin Hogg the rather pathetic plea: 'ΜΗΔΕΝ' ΑΓΑΝ' (nothing to excess).

Powell returned to the subject in a speech to the Rotary Club at Eastbourne the following month (16 November). He gave a few more examples of the intimidation of an old lady by coloured men, which, though identified, did not satisfy newspaper investigators. The *News of the World,* for instance, which supported Powell's politics to the hilt, greeted his examples with the reproving headline: 'THIS WON'T DO ENOCH'.

Powell came to the point – the 'key significance of repatriation or re-emigration'. Too many people, complained Powell, in an implied reference to Heath, were underestimating the importance of this part of Conservative policy.

'I believe,' he said,

that ignorance of the realities of Commonwealth immigration leads people seriously to underestimate the scope of the policy and thus to neglect and despise the *chief key* to the situation.

In order to justify this sudden emphasis on repatriation, Powell ended his speech on a theme which had been scrupulously avoided by Conservative leaders in the past: the theme of pollution. Already, he argued, even if all immigration was stopped immediately, the situation was intolerable. The immigrants were too many and too alien to be assimilable. Four years earlier, when there were one million coloured people in

Britain, Powell had said that he would always 'set his face like flint against making any difference between one citizen of this country and another on grounds of his origin'. Now, when there were approximately one million, two hundred thousand immigrants in the country he could tell the Eastbourne Rotarians:

The West Indian or Indian does not, by being born in England, become an Englishman. In law he becomes a United Kingdom citizen by birth; in fact he is a West Indian or an Asian still.

If the Indians and West Indians in Britain were more than a 'tiny minority', Powell's argument continued, the nation would suffer. The theme of national disaster was deliberately played upon by reference to poetic clichés – clichés which in this context had interesting antecedents.

This theme, like the stories of old ladies terrorized and raped by excreta-throwing blacks, had been used to some extent by propaganda which, before Powell spoke, had been regarded as undignified.

According to the British National Party publication, *Combat*, of March/April 1961, a debate in the House of Commons

gave the opportunity for such pale pink Tory pansies as Nigel Fisher and the racial degenerates of the Bow Group entourage to vent their spleen against proposals that would retard the march to build a mulatto state in England's 'green and pleasant land'.

The British National Party *Colour Quiz* two years later, asked:

Is it right that England's green and pleasant land should be turned into a black slum? (*Combat*, March/April 1963).

Sir Oswald Mosley's Union Movement uttered the same warning:

The coming of 1984 will find a mongrel Britain. Do the rank and file of the Labour Party want this – everything they fought for, England's green and pleasant land, turned into a 20th century Tower of Babel? (*Action*, 25 October 1963).

And, finally, from *Combat* again:

With a million already here, and breeding three times as fast as our own people, how long will it be until Birmingham, England, becomes Birmingham, Alabama? (May/June, 1963).

Some five years later, Powell reverted to the same theme:

Time is running against us and them. With the lapse of a generation or so we shall at last have succeeded in reproducing in 'England's green and pleasant land' the haunting tragedy of the United States.

The assembling of these quotations is not an exercise in establishing guilt by association. On the contrary, if Powell was right at Eastbourne in 1968, then all the other quotations were right at the time they were used. For Powell cannot legitimately argue that the numbers of immigrants in 1963 or 1964 were any more assimilable in future generations than they were in 1968. The difference between the two sets of figures is of negligible significance to future generations. If it was true in 1968 that 'England's green and pleasant land' would in future years be damaged by immigrants and their 'offspring' (Powell's delightful word for children), then the same was true in 1963. Moreover, the warnings from *Combat* and *Action* in 1963 were based on the same proposition; namely that there was something about the coloured man which was intrinsically different: that a coloured child born and bred in England could not become an Englishman but remained forever, essentially different: that, in Powell's words (at Birmingham),

whatever drawbacks attended the immigrants ... arose from those personal circumstances and accidents which cause, *and always will cause* the fortunes and experiences of one man to be different from another's.

In 1963 the demands of *Combat* and *Action* were regarded by almost all leading Conservatives, and most others, as non-sensical racialism. Conservative leaders at that time argued that black children born in England could and would grow up as indistinguishable in every aspect apart from colour to white children, provided that efforts were made to outlaw racial discrimination. The arguments of the British National Party about coloured immigrants were boycotted by most

Conservatives on the grounds that they encouraged the racial divisions which they wrongly predicted as inevitable. It was the singular achievement of Enoch Powell to bring these formerly boycotted and discredited arguments out of the murky backwaters of extremism into the mainstream of British politics.

Powell's Eastbourne speech was greeted with even more fury than his Birmingham speech the previous April. Edward Heath, speaking at Folkestone, condemned it as 'character assassination of one racial group' and remarked: 'That way lies tyranny.' Heath was echoed by many other Conservative leaders, but, only two months later, Heath travelled to Walsall, there to deliver another speech on immigration, and move his Party's policy still further to the right.

At Walsall, Heath demanded new legislation by August 1969, preventing new immigrants from permanent settlement; that they should be admitted 'for a specific job in a specific place – for a specific time'. Each immigrant's permit would 'have to be renewed every year, and their permit would have to be renewed every time they want to move to another job'. Moreover, 'future immigrants should no longer enjoy an absolute right to bring their relatives, however close'.

The most accurate reaction to this speech came from the audience, one of whom asked, to thunderous applause:

May I say how delighted we are that Mr Heath appears to have adopted many of the views expressed by Enoch Powell?

Despite Heath's feeble protestations, this was clearly the right analysis. Even at York, Heath had not spelt out a policy of second class citizenship quite so crudely. All the previous talk about treating immigrants as equal citizens was now thrown out of the window. They should be allowed in in future, suggested Heath, as factory fodder, with no right to be joined by their families, no right to move around the country freely, no right even to stay as long as they wished. As soon as their job vanished, so would they. Small wonder that this retreat by the Conservative leader was greeted with a standing ovation by the faithful. And small wonder that the television cameras concentrated throughout the standing ovation on the awkward figure of Enoch Powell, rising and clapping as earnestly as anyone in the hall.

Heath was shortly to discover what others had discovered before him: that concessions to racialist and anti-immigration demands inspire more demands. Three weeks after the Walsall speech, Mr Duncan Sandys, on 12 February, tried to bring in a Bill in the Commons for the further control of Commonwealth immigration. The speech followed Heath's Walsall proposals closely, but went slightly further by limiting the right of entry of dependants of immigrants already here.

126 Conservatives voted for the Bill, which was defeated by a majority of 121. Among those voting for it were Sir Alec Douglas Home, Mr William Whitelaw, the Tory Chief Whip, most of the executive of the 1922 Committee, and about twenty former junior Ministers. Heath, Maudling and Macleod abstained and thus brought themselves into still further derision in the eyes of their rank and file. As the *Sunday Telegraph* (16 February 1969) put it:

Powellites are claiming a major victory in shifting the party leadership far over to the right and in support of the Powell/Sandys line on immigration.

As the months went on, however, there was again a temporary lull in discussion of the immigration problem, and a lull in the discussion of it by Enoch Powell. This deficiency was duly made up by another major speech on the subject, proclaimed with the same advance publicity – at Wolverhampton on 9 June.

The speech started with a flood of statistics about children: the percentages of coloured children in the schools of immigrant areas, and the percentage of births to immigrant mothers. In this section, Powell dropped any pretence that he was concerned with immigration as such, and made it quite plain that he was worried only about coloured immigration. The references are to 'white' births and 'non-white areas'.

The facts which he produced would, he said, 'have been thought blankly incredible only a year or two ago and would have been derided if they had been predicted.'

If, in 1963 or 1964, a statistician had said:

> About 5 per cent of the people of this borough are immigrants, but, because none of them are old people and very few of them are children, they constitute about 20 per cent of the child-bearing population. If you allow them to bring over their wives and cohabit with them, you can expect that about a quarter of the children born here will be black, and about a quarter of the children in the schools will be black

would he really have been derided? Was it really 'blankly incredible' that, to take the most sensational of Mr Powell's figures, more than half the children in Southall's primary schools were black or brown, when for nearly twenty years Indian and Pakistani workers had been flooding into Southall to man the light industries which had grown up in the industrial complex around London airport?

Statisticians and politicians had not asked these obvious questions nor made these obvious predictions – not because the problem was not foreseeable, but because attitudes at that time were very different. The attitude was not: how can we terrify the rabble with predictions of a black takeover? but, how best can we deal with the problems created by inevitable large-scale immigration of people from different backgrounds?

That was why politicians like Enoch Powell acquired a reputation for being 'extremely hostile to bringing race into politics' and why politicians like Powell proclaimed in headlines: 'INTEGRATION – THE ONLY WAY'. That was why politicians like Powell on the very few occasions when they applied themselves to the numbers of coloured children thought, not how many there were likely to be in twenty years' time, but how, on the contrary, however many there were, they could be properly integrated in the community.

As late as December 1967, in a radio broadcast on the BBC Overseas Service, which, no doubt, Powell thought would not come to the attention of his constituents, Powell replied to Mr Anthony Lester, a barrister who specializes in community relations, who had argued the importance of creating a climate in which coloured children born in Britain could feel themselves part of one community . . .

'If you're going to come in again Anthony,' Powell said,

123

I would like to agree with you about one thing. And that is I do agree that the real problem is the children – I'm absolutely with you about that – it is the way in which the children born in this country are going to find their place in our society, and all that I say and think about further amendment of the immigration laws is very much with a view to the way in which those children will be embodied in the community.

Less than a year after this self-righteousness, Powell was saying at Eastbourne that a child born in England of West Indian or Asian parents did not become an Englishman. Now, only eighteen months later, he was devoting a large part of a long speech to emphasizing the differences between coloured children and white children and the 'dangerous menace' which their numbers presented. The children of whom he spoke so warmly to African listeners on the BBC Overseas Service were now referred to as 'alien here, yet homeless elsewhere'. These children were 'alien here' and presumably always 'alien here' because of the colour of their skin.

This was the preamble to the real point of Powell's speech: to increase his demands still further, to raise the bid in the auction into which he had entered eighteen months previously. In April, at Birmingham, he had broken the sound barrier of ordinary controversy by giving credence to racialist gossip, and had called for stiffer controls on immigrants' entry; in October, at the Party Conference, he had stressed the importance of the Party's programme on repatriation, a theme which he developed in his 'green and pleasant land' speech at Eastbourne. Now, in June 1969, he emphasized repatriation still further and even proposed a separate Ministry to deal with repatriation. He referred only in passing to the need for stricter controls. What mattered, he said, was repatriation – which was 'by the far the most important' part of Conservative policy. The pledge to repatriate was of 'extreme urgency and importance'. And, therefore, after quoting some highly dubious statistics about how many immigrants wanted to be repatriated, Powell demonstrated how his repatriation operation could be carried out. It would be voluntary, based on a financial subvention to immigrants willing to return home.

Financially if one estimates that 600,000 to 700,000 would be involved, and that the average size of family is five, then to give each family £2,000 for passage and resettlement would cost £260m. Raise this to £300m. to include all the costs of administration etc. and it would still represent only the cost of eighteen months' aid to underdeveloped countries, at the present rate, and it is hard to imagine a more effective or realistic form of 'aid' than this transfusion not only of finance but also of skill, experience and education.

The idea and the comparison were not original. In its April/June 1964 edition, *Combat*, the organ of the British National Party, had outlined its policy:

We advocate as a first step that fares home, and resettlement grants where necessary, should be paid to all immigrants wishing to return to their lands of origin and including those born here of immigrant stock. At an average fare of £70 per person to the West Indies, India or Africa, this would still cost less than the money we give away each year as 'aid to the underdeveloped countries'.

The further two 'steps' advocated at that time by the BNP were:
1. the banning of all National Assistance to those immigrants who refused to go and
2. an attractive financial grant to all coloured people willing to undertake voluntary sterilization.

Having expressed in detail his policy for repatriation, Powell for the first time in any of his speeches, openly attacked Mr Edward Heath. He singled out Heath's speech at Walsall the previous January, which he described as 'sheer incomprehension of the very magnitude of the danger itself'.

Yet it was the Walsall speech which Powell had cheered so enthusiastically, joining in the standing ovation with decisive and deliberate enthusiasm. It was after the Walsall speech that Heath was congratulated in the audience for 'moving towards the policies of Mr Enoch Powell'. It was the Walsall speech which was widely regarded in the newspapers as a decisive shift to incorporate Powellism in official policy.

Was Powell applauding 'sheer incomprehension' at Walsall? Was he so much a hypocrite that he could leap to his feet and clap his leader for a speech which he regarded as missing the major point, and laying the nation open to a 'dangerous menace'? Probably not. More probably, at the time of Heath's Walsall speech, Powell agreed with it. Six months later, he could no longer agree with it if he was to stay in the game of Immigration Poker, in which players must raise the bid every time their contestant plays. The game of Immigration Poker in major parties is likely to go on for several months yet, with Mr Heath desperately trying to match Powell's bids and force him to throw in his hand.

Of all the reactions to Mr Powell's three major speeches on immigration in 1968 and 1969, none were more fascinating than those of the extreme right. Sir Oswald Mosley's Union Movement immediately denounced Powell as an opportunist, demonstrating in its literature that Mosley had said everything Powell was saying at least nine years before. This demonstrated the extent to which the Union Movement had been overtaken on the extreme right by other organizations who knew a good chance when they saw one. The National Front, for instance, which was formed in 1967 as a result of a merger between the British National Party, the Greater Britain Movement, the League of Empire Loyalists and the Racial Preservation Society, came out in instant support of Powell. The leader in *Combat* was entitled, 'Our Debt to Powell'. Mr A. K. Chesterton, policy director of the National Front, told *The Times* (24 April 1968):

What Mr Powell has said does not vary in any way from our view.

Mr Robert Taylor, who was at the time Sheffield organizer of the National Front, but has since resigned, told me that the Huddersfield branch of the National Front was built almost entirely on the strength of support for Powell's speeches. 'We held a march,' he says,

in Huddersfield in support of what Powell had said, and we signed eight people up as members of the branch that afternoon. Powell's speeches gave our membership and morale a tremendous boost. Before Powell spoke, we were getting only cranks and perverts. After his speeches we started to attract, in a secret sort of way, the right-wing members of the Tory organizations.

Perhaps the most revealing comment of all on the Powell speeches came from John Tyndall, editor of *Spearhead*, the 'theoretical' journal of the National Front:

The time is 1958. Race problems have just started to make themselves felt in Britain. A few souls venture to reply that race problems are not the fault of racialists, but in fact the fault of those who are standing smugly by while a huge coloured population builds up in Britain. Those few predict that the answer is not 'integration', nor the throwing of abuse at race-conscious whites, but to stop the flood and redirect the immigrants home, in their own interests as much as in ours.

Now, coming forward ten years to 1968, it is well to recall these days, and to remember who those few men were. Among the gentlemen n Parliament, the lone voice of warning was that of Sir Cyril Osborne, the member for Louth. Outside Parliament, those who spoke out were regarded as even lower.

Who were they? One was John Bean, editor of *Combat*. Another was A. K. Chesterton, now leader of the National Front. And, let us be fair, two others, although we may disagree with the rest of their politics, were Sir Oswald Mosley and Colin Jordan. Among many others in a lesser role was your present editor.

Nothing had yet been heard from Enoch Powell on the subject.

That Mr Enoch Powell has now spoken out is to be welcomed.

But let us not forget those who uttered the warning long, long, ago.

John Tyndall had a point. He and his colleagues in his roll of honour had about them a certain ghoulish consistency. As soon as the first black men started to land in Britain, Tyndall and his colleagues started shouting for them to be sent home.

Enoch Powell, however, could claim no such consistency. His insistence that 'numbers are of the essence' in immigration matters is not born out by his own record in speeches on the subject. His demands for immigration control and repatriation do not rise and fall with the numbers of immigrants. They rise and fall according to the political atmosphere and the likelihood of political advantage. In 1958–60 and in 1963–4, in both of which periods there was large scale Commonwealth immigration, Enoch Powell did not refer to the issue. In 1966, with the exception of a few half-hearted comments at election time, he was silent on the matter. In all these periods, the political atmosphere was not conducive to demands for further controls and repatriation schemes

Similarly, as Powell's demands come to be satisfied, so he increases them. First he demanded more immigration control by labour vouchers. When more control by voucher was introduced in 1965, he demanded control of Kenyan Asians. When the Kenyan Asians were controlled in 1968, he emphasized control of dependants. As the number of dependants began to drop, he demanded repatriation, first incidentally, then as 'a matter of great urgency'.

Of all the comments on Mr Powell's rise to fame as a result of his 1968 and 1969 speeches on immigration and race, none was more accurate than that of a close colleague of Mr Powell's for many years, Lord Lambton, Conservative M.P. for Berwick. Writing three days after Powell's first speech, Lambton, who has always been regarded as a right-wing Conservative, struck at the root of Powell's motivation:

His speech should not be regarded in isolation, but as part of a planned policy, which he has followed since the retirement of Mr Macmillan. Ever since, he has believed sincerely that he was the right man to lead the Conservative Party.

What he is saying, in effect, to the country – having chosen a popular cause – is:

'I am the man to lead you. I am the man alone of the Conservative leaders today who understands what people in this country want and take this opportunity of proving to you by risking my whole career to prove it.' (*Express and Star*, 24 April 1968).

The truth was that this 'austere' politician, who over more than twenty years of public life had established for himself a reputation for altruism and integrity, had embarked on one of the most dangerous and opportunist escapades in the history of British politics.

Chapter 4
Weasel Words

In a private speech to lobby correspondents before his big speeches on immigration, Powell revealed the true source of his political inspiration.

Often, when I am kneeling down in church, I think to myself how much we should thank God, the Holy Ghost, for the gift of capitalism. (quoted in *Enoch Powell: The Man and his Thinking* by T. E. Utley, p. 114).

During the war, in India, Powell was a confirmed atheist, yet even his atheism was rooted in a belief in a supernatural providence which provided immortal wonders such as Monarchy and Empire. To interfere in any way with such wonders was to tilt at providence. So, too, with capitalism. For Enoch Powell, the drive for profit and the resulting division of society into classes is the dynamic which will generate the maximum benefit for everyone concerned. It is this system which can best ensure the defeat of all human evils, even the evil of racial discrimination. 'Perhaps,' wrote Powell in the summer of 1964,

the Free World has too long denied itself the right to proclaim that the market economy which it opposes to communism is the most effective enemy of discrimination between individuals, classes and races. (*Sunday Times*, 14 June 1964).

In the course of his many discourses in favour of the free market system, Powell has often referred to the need to establish a free market in that most valuable and most complex of capitalism's commodities: labour. 'The essence of socialism,' he had told his constituents, 'is to prevent the customer determining the free flow of labour and materials, and, instead, to plan from the centre.' In the spring of 1964, he launched an attack on the concept of regional planning: of 'attracting industry' away from the South East towards the development areas of relatively high unemployment, like Scotland and the North East.

'Such a policy,' he said,

if adopted at any past point of time which one cares to name, would have inhibited severely those movements of labour and industry which in retrospect are recognized to have been essential to economic progress. *There is no past pattern of the distribution of employment in Great Britain which could have been 'frozen' without economic loss or even disaster.* (Speech at Glasgow, 3 April 1964).

In an article entitled 'More Freedom to Move to a Job', Powell wrote:

Instead of trying to reverse economic trends, might it not be better to reinforce them by helping and encouraging the man who needs a job to move to the place where someone is anxious to employ him? . . .

If labour were freer to move, there would obviously be less variation in unemployment between one region and another. So, in seeking a cure for excessive variation, the most natural thing to do first is to look for the obstacles to movement and think how to lessen or remove them. (*Sunday Telegraph*, 3 May 1964).

In another article, Powell welcomed the results of the free market in labour mobility in Britain:

Concentration of population and activity in large and dense aggregations is an essential concomitant of economic progress. What we denigrate as 'congestion' in the South East may be among the greatest assets – there are precious few natural ones – of what we are pleased to call 'this overcrowded island'. (*Sunday Telegraph*, 22 March 1964).

Powell went on to argue that, if labour was allowed to move freely according to the availability of jobs, the services for that labour would be best provided where the jobs were. He ridiculed the conservatism of Scottish workers, and their 'unspoken prejudice against mobility'. He urged that houses, schools, hospitals, transport and the like would automatically become more available in those areas where employers decided they wished to set up 'concentrations of industry'.

These ideas were responsible for the lack of political planning or provision for the mass immigration into London and the Midlands of Scotsmen, Irishmen, West Indians and Asians

130

in the post-war years of economic growth. The concentration of industry in these areas required a regular flow of labour, and the supply from Scotland and Ireland was not enough. The additional labour came from the Commonwealth. Its coming was entirely unplanned, yet the Conservative Government welcomed and sanctioned it because the employers wanted the labour.

The second part of the Powell formula, was however, swiftly disproved. The magic of the free enterprise system produced the workers to man its industries – but it could not produce even the most essential services for those workers. The factories were working overtime, but there were not enough houses, schools, hospitals, transport, social security benefits. These shortages dated back as long as anyone could remember, but, as the new workers came in, so the indigenous workers started to blame them for the shortages. 'We have not enough houses to house our own people,' was the popular cry. 'Why do we let in all these people to make the housing situation worse?'

In fact, the shortages in the social services had nothing to do with the immigration. The most concise statement of this is in the Milner Holland Report on London Housing of 1965, which Powell has cited in his favour.

In a section dealing with 'popular hypotheses' the Report examines the view that

the migration to London of people from other parts of the country, and particularly from overseas, has created the worst housing conditions and these could be eliminated by stricter control of immigration.

The Report replies:

Immigrants come to London in search of work – and find it, for we have seen no evidence that they are more frequently unemployed or dependent on National Assistance than others in similar occupations. If they did not come, either their places would be taken by migrants from other parts of the country, or a large number of essential jobs would remain unfilled. *The plight of the immigrant is the outcome, and too often an extreme example, of London's housing difficulties; it is not their cause.* (Milner Holland Report, Cmnd. 2605: pp. 202, 203).

The point is rammed home statistically in a powerful article by Mrs K. Jones in the *Economic Review* of August 1967, entitled 'Immigrants and the Social Services'. The article produces the following table,* which shows that in every area of social welfare the cost per head is higher for the total population than it is for the immigrant population.

Cost per head of the Social Services, 1961-1981

£ at 1961 prices

	Health and Welfare	Education and Child Care	National Insurance and Assistance Benefits	Total
1961				
Total population	18·5	12·4	31·2	62·1
Immigrant population	18·4	13·3	19·2	50·9
1966				
Total population	18·6	12·1	31·7	62·4
Immigrant population	17·4	13·9	17·4	48·7
1981				
Total population	19·0	15·3	33·5	67·8
A. Immigrant[2] population	16·9	21·6	19·1	57·6
B. Immigrant[3] population	16·8	22·9	18·1	57·9

1. Current expenditure and grants.
2. Assuming no further net immigration.
3. Assuming some continued immigration.

'The average immigrant,' Mrs Jones concludes,

received about 80 per cent as much [in social benefit] as the average member of the total population in 1961, and the figure seems likely to be 80–85 per cent in 1981.

The adult working population supports the old in the community. An inflow of young adult immigrants therefore – so far as current

---

* Reproduced from the *National Institute Economic Review* No. 41, August 1967.

expenditure on the social services is concerned – provides a once-for-all gain for some thirty years, in which they add to the contributors, but not to the dependants. This fact more than outweighs the additional social service current costs which may be incurred because of immigrants' special health or educational requirements.

Mrs Jones goes further than Milner Holland. Milner Holland shows that immigration is not the cause of the housing shortage. Mrs Jones says that immigrants' contribution to the social services is greater than that of the total population. In other words, without immigration the social service shortages would be greater, not less.

These facts teach us something about Mr Powell's free market economy. It delivers workers to the employer – any number of workers he requires; but it does not deliver the services for the workers. Full employment, expansion, a booming capitalism still does not provide decent housing, schools, welfare services for its workers. Immigration or not, housing shortages, overcrowded schools, inadequate old age pensions, insanitary and insufficient hospitals are an integral part of the capitalism for which Mr Powell thanks the Holy Ghost. Immigrants attracted by the pull of that market suffer, together with indigenous workers, from these shortages. In no way do they create them or even aggravate them.

Powell's attitude to the greatest and most serious of these shortages – the housing shortage – is to leave it to the free market. He was one of the chief architects of the Rent Act of 1957 which took a large stock of privately-owned houses out of the jurisdiction of the Rent Restriction Acts, thus allowing landlords to charge whatever they wished. The Act also 'decontrolled' property vacated by tenants in occupation at the time of the Act. This 'creeping decontrol' encouraged landlords to rid their property of sitting tenants.

'There was no prouder moment in my life,' Powell once told his constituents,

than when I rose in November 1956 to read the second reading of the Rent Bill which began the dismantling of the restrictions on private housing that was to strike the shackles off the only force that could house people as it met all their other needs – enterprise and competition. (*Express and Star*, 8 October 1964).

Powell's speech on the Rent Bill made three main predictions about the housing market after the decontrol of rented property proposed by the Bill had taken place. There would, he said, be an increase in rented property because 'the inducement of an owner to attempt to get the current value of his house by selling it will disappear'.

Secondly,

houses will no longer be held empty month after month waiting for a purchase. Those houses will not be let because in future there will be no difference between the value of the house with vacant possession and the house with tenants.

Thirdly,

the Bill will halt the drain upon rented accommodation; it will release additional accommodation which is under-used or wasted; it will arrest the deterioration of houses for lack of maintenance; and it will give to persons who are moving or setting up home the opportunity to find accommodation on the market. (Hansard, 21 November 1956).

None of these things happened. In 1960, the Tory Government produced a White Paper on the effects of the Rent Act in its first three years' operation. (Rent Act, Report of Inquiry, Cmnd. 1246).

According to this Report, under-occupation had increased. 'There has,' it reported, 'been a slight increase in the number of rateable units which might be considered to be under-occupied.' The number of rented houses had declined. Of the 317,000 houses decontrolled in 1957, only 237,000 remained rented. The trend to owner-occupation increased. 12 per cent of all those houses decontrolled in 1957 had become owner-occupied. There was no measurable increase in the amount of accommodation put out to let by owner-occupiers (p. 20) and, finally, there were many more empty houses. Table 1 (p. 17) of the Report, showed more vacancies for every type of house. The symmetry of Enoch Powell's logic had been shattered by the greed and selfishness of the landlords.

All these trends continued until 1964, negating every one of Powell's original predictions. Conservative Ministers were not a little embarrassed about their Rent Act and kept very quiet about it in the 1964 election campaign. When the Labour

Government promptly repealed the Act, there was no opposition from the Tory front bench. Only Powell, for whom ideology has always been more important than fact, could proclaim to this constituents that he was proud to have introduced the most regressive social legislation since the war.

The Conservatives' Rent Act hit the immigrant especially hard. The overall shortage of rented accommodation was aggravated by the discrimination of private landlords. Immigrants were forced to buy dilapidated houses at high mortgage rates. As Milner Holland put it (p. 195):

Although coloured immigrants are in great demand in London for manning many of its services, they are one of the groups who have the greatest difficulty in securing satisfactory housing accommodation.

The 'creeping de-control' provisions of Powell's Rent Act encouraged landlords to get rid of controlled tenants so that the law of the market could prevail, and Peter Rachman became the champion of the free market in Notting Hill. Gangsters and terrorists, white and coloured, flourished in the free housing market, the creation of which was the proudest moment in Enoch Powell's life.

As for other social services – hospital beds, places in schools, child care and so on – even Enoch Powell does not argue that these would be more plentiful under private enterprise. That there are hospital beds and schools at all for 'low-income' groups is due to the 'interference' of the State in the free play of the market.

In the process of post-war immigration to Britain, what did Powell's private enterprise market system provide? With its Rent Act, it provided less privately-rented houses for low-income groups. It provided no hospitals, no schools, almost no transport. It provided no planning whereby people from different backgrounds could be more easily assimilated in the indigenous community, no race relation commissions, no extra welfare services, language lessons, teacher-training courses for teaching overseas children. It provided no dispersal of industry to avoid the conglomeration of immigrants in the conurbations, no urban planning to avoid their dispersal within the conurbations. It provided no method of avoiding the use of immigrant labour as cheap labour. New workers without services: that was the contribution of the free market system to the post-war British economy. And when the combination led, inevitably, to resentment against the new workers, Enoch Powell and the other supporters of the free market were the first to sympathize with and encourage it to their political advantage.

For the real problems which confront immigrants and their neighbours, Enoch Powell has no credible solution. His solution to the housing problem is to do away with rent control (the only means yet discovered of ensuring accommodation at low rent for low-income groups), and with council housing subsidies (the means by which council housing at reasonable rent comes to be built and occupied). Powell's remedies for housing would have the immediate effect of almost completely dispensing with the available accommodation for 'low-income groups', and of reducing the building programme for council houses. In all other fields of social service, education, health and so on, Powell's remedies seek to improve conditions for a wealthy few and make them worse for the masses: thus further increasing tension between immigrants and their neighbours. Confronted with the deep divide between the industrial and underdeveloped countries, one of the main reasons for immigration, Powell proposes an abolition of all aid to underdeveloped countries, and its replacement by 'trade'.

Solutions for the real problems must be left entirely to the laws of the free market, but solutions for the unreal problems, the racial problems, are quite different. Suddenly the High Priest of Free Enterprise proposes rigid restrictionism and control. The free market in labour has, he says, to be frustrated. The scourge of bureaucracy in Whitehall proposes a new Ministry of Repatriation; the man who grudges every penny of expenditure of public money on housing, schools or hospitals, blandly proposes expenditure of £300m. to send the blacks home.

Powell does not emphasize the argument that immigration is a strain on the social services. What worries Powell is the racial aspect.

As he says, in a quotation which has been used more than once in preceding chapters:

The West Indian or Asian does not, by being born in England become an Englishman. In law, he becomes a United Kingdom citizen by birth; in fact, he is a West Indian or Asian still.

What is it that makes him 'a West Indian or Asian still'? It cannot be his origin, for he was born in this country; nor his environment, nor his education, nor his language, nor even his accent. What distinguishes the 'West Indian or Asian born in England' from the English child is his colour.

At a lecture on Nationalism at a Conservative Political Centre summer school in 1955, Powell explained that

the principle of majority decision is divisive: it splits a society along its natural lines of fission into the sections sufficiently homogenous for all their members to accept the will of the majority as their own . . .

'The line of fission,' Powell went on,

may be racial, provided that difference of race, in the absence of religious or linguistic differences, is marked by plain and visible distinctions, such as colour; *for men assume that those who look differently from themselves have different interests* – there could scarcely have been anti-Semitism as we have known it unless Jews were recognizable at sight. ('World Perspectives', Conservative Political Centre, 1955: p. 39.)

Powell does not say whether 'men' are right 'to assume' that people who looked differently 'have different interests', but there is no other explanation for the statement that the 'West Indian or Indian does not, by being born in England become an Englishman'.

On 29 January 1902, Major William Evans Gordon, Tory M.P. for Stepney, moved an Amendment to the King's Speech demanding control of Jewish aliens coming into Britain. He did not have the statistical flair of Enoch Powell, but he warned the Commons that with the continued influx of Jews into the East End of London,

it is only a matter of time before the population becomes entirely foreign.

Yes, foreign. For, as Evans Gordon might have put it:

'The Jew does not by being born in England become an Englishman.... He is a Jew still.' Enoch Powell is saying exactly the same about a new group of immigrants. All that has changed is that new scapegoats must be found for the homelessness, the bad hospital conditions, and the overcrowded schools created by the politics and parties of Evans Gordon and Enoch Powell. To preserve the bogus notion that the interests of William Evans Gordon and Enoch Powell are the same as those they represent, it is necessary to foster the illusion in men's minds that 'those who look differently to themselves have different interests'.

The comparison between Powell and Evans Gordon extends further. Evans Gordon's support grew with every attack on Jewish immigration but despite requests to found a separate anti-immigration Party, he remained a 'High Tory' throughout.

Eventually, however, after the election of a Liberal Government in 1906, and after a few more racialist tirades, Evans Gordon vanished from the limelight.

Enoch Powell is a more substantial figure in his Party than was Evans Gordon, but he may well, for rather different reasons, fail as dismally to reach the pinnacles of political power.

The extent of Powell's popularity in the country is based chiefly on his attitude towards race. Before his race speeches, his following was comparatively small and no one seriously judged him a future Tory leader.

Yet the mantle of populist leader, seized so eagerly, fits badly on Powell. On the subject of immigration, he plays the demagogue brilliantly, asserting that he speaks for 'ordinary, decent people'; assuring his audiences that his enemies are out to 'destroy society as we know it'; dispensing gaily with awkward statistics; reflecting constantly that here is something rotten in the State which must be cut out. (For an interesting comparison between Powell's language and that of the late Senator Joe McCarthy, see Peter Jenkins, 'The McCarthy in our midst', *Guardian*, 13 June 1969.)

Yet common to all good populist leaders of the right has been the ability to be vague on social issues. National Socialism promised more houses, better social conditions and better pensions once the main issues, those of the Jews and of national regeneration, had been dealt with. National Socialist politics and pledges were racially specific and politically vague. McCarthy had no detailed solution to the economic or political problems of the day. All would sort itself out, he implied, once the Communist had been smoked out of the State Department. Joseph Chamberlain, father-figure of Midland Conservatism, based his appeal on a vague protectionism – a call for keeping out foreign goods and foreign workers – coupled with pledges of State-sponsored social reform and welfare benefits.

Enoch Powell, on the other hand, is specific about everything. He wants to cut housing subsidies and rent control. He unashamedly attacks trade unionists. He even attacks the Backing Britain Movement. His position (this metaphor I owe to Malcolm Muggeridge) is that of a womanizer, eager to taste each woman in full, swearing himself true to every one, but unable, in the last resort, to commit himself to any one for fear of losing the others. He is a politician who dabbles in too many issues too often to avoid making major mistakes. The friends he makes out of one campaign are made enemies by the next one.

Secondly, more importantly, the times are not ripe for populist leaders.

In a speech at Gloucester in 1967, Enoch Powell touched on a raw political nerve: the widespread confusion and cynicism about politics.

The citizen is told that he has failed in comparison with the citizens of other nations; that he ought to be 'growing' one, two, three per cent faster than he is; that he ought to be exporting more, not less; and finally (the crowning insult) that he is not paying his way in the world. Night and day, through the months and years, a babel of voices dins these unintelligible moral denunciations into the heads of ordinary English men and women, for whom they bear not the slightest relationship to any of the facts of their daily existence.... Some time there has to be an end to this. Some time – and why not now? – the citizen will put his faith again in the great simplicities and will confound the merchants o mumbo-jumbo.

Much of this is true. The exhortations about the balance

of payments have long since ceased to have any meaning or relevance to the reality of people's lives. Yet the answer to his question 'Why not Now?', when asking for a day when the citizen will 'once again put his faith in the great simplicities' is that there is nothing much in it for the citizen. During the Weimar Republic in inter-war Germany, the 'great simplicities' of the right – notably Jewish complicity in national degeneration – were substitutes for unemployment, slump, national humiliation at an armistice, the past property and glories of a dispossessed and frightened bourgeoisie. The great, and monstrous 'simplicities' filled, as they were intended to fill, a genuine vacuum in people's lives.

Today, the vacuum on the right is only political. The 'great simplicities' of the right are politically attractive, but not materially so. Politics may be humbug, but profits are rising, as are share and property values. If the 'small man' is perplexed by the power of monopolies, he can still take out profitable investments to compensate him for his lack of prestige. Unemployment is negligible, the gross national product continues to rise, and, even if politicians and politics are widely debased, there is as yet no material case for reverting to the 'great simplicities'.

Yet there can be no underestimating the impact and the significance of Powell's excursion into the greatest of the 'great simplicities' – the campaign against coloured immigration. His campaign has altered the dimensions of political debate in Britain. Open attacks on coloured people and their presence in Britain are now part of respectable political controversy. If economic growth and boom give way to economic insecurity and unemployment and if the grip of the consensus is relaxed, there is no limit to the potential of the politics of Enoch Powell.

For this easy rise to fame, Powell's alleged opponents are, at least to some extent, responsible. These include not only the Conservative leaders, who have reacted to each Powell initiative by abhorring it and then responding to it. They include, perhaps even more centrally, the Labour Government, which has responded to demands and pressures from the anti-immigrant right by conceding to them. Ironically, this policy has not even brought with it electoral advantage. Labour's standing in the country and among its own supporters did not drop as a result of its stand against the Commonwealth Immigrants Bill in 1961 and 1962. On the contrary, the Party started to recover after the 1959 election defeat, and to make substantial gains in by-elections, some of them in immigrant areas.

From achieving office in 1964, however, Labour retreated from its 1961 position, and meekly surrendered to each new resurgence of demands for immigration control. In August 1965, they introduced a White Paper restricting immigration which was, among other things, blatantly contradictory to their own National Plan. Even less justifiable was the Commonwealth Immigrants Act, 1968, passed as a new chorus of anti-immigrant demands was rising to a crescendo. Had these new cries been met with fierce Government opposition, they might well have been silenced. Had the full force of the Labour movement and the Government been thrown behind an anti-racialist campaign and a firm pledge to keep their promises to the Kenyan Asians, the vacuum into which Powell smartly moved would never have been created. As it was, the speed with which the Government collapsed before the Sandys/Powell offensive encouraged the latter to continue on the attack.

Even after the Kenyan Asians Bill, the Government continued to backslide, introducing further controls by banning fiancées of immigrants already here, and, more seriously still, insisting that dependants who want to join immigrants in Britain should acquire an entry certificate in their own country. This apparently plausible restriction meant that Indian and Pakistani families have had and will have to suffer delays of several months before joining their husbands. And some of them, as a result of this restriction and the inefficient bureaucracy of birth registrations in India, will never get in at all.

On 10 March 1969, Harold Wilson spoke at a 20th anniversary dinner of the Jewish Vanguard, and addressed himself to the 'evil' of Powellism. After a few well-received attacks on racialism, he went on:

Nor is this manifestation of what I can only describe as evil confined to those who openly seize on race problems for political purposes. It is no less evil when it takes the form of weasel words of those who seek political profit by pretending to go along with the leaders of racialism, while inserting sufficient in small print to be able to say afterwards that they had not said it, or that they had said nothing new.

This was, of course, a reference to Edward Heath, and a fair one. But the sense of it applied equally well to Harold Wilson. Heath had used weasel words, but Wilson and his Government had indulged in weasel action. While Wilson attacked Powell verbally, his Government hastened to put into practice the demands which Powell was making.

This was not only the work of the large band of opportunists, has-beens and James Callaghans in the Labour Government. As shown in the previous chapter, the Government had initiated a period of progressive race relations. This period – from the autumn of 1965 to the autumn of 1967 – saw the birth of the extended Race Relations Bill, the proliferation of community relations committees throughout the country, multi-racial housing associations, language classes and so on. These initiatives were largely the work of the Labour Government's most trenchant liberal, Mr Roy Jenkins.

After a token resistance, however, the 'liberals' in the Labour Cabinet have crumbled almost as fast as the opportunists, with the results that two years of painstaking and successful race relations work was torn to shreds by a single speech from Enoch Powell.

The most significant characteristic of these liberals was their elitism. They had gone about their race relations work quietly and in private, without seeking to disturb the public. They had met in the Home Office, or in the homes of committee chairmen to plan their next housing association or English language class. They had sought, to use Powell's metaphor, to 'catch their monkey softly'. In a period of few public statements about racialism, and where the Government enjoyed the complete cooperation of the official Opposition, these quiet liberals scored some notable successes, as the public opinion polls of the time about improving race relations demonstrate.

Powell's speech swept all this aside, and, to their horror,

the liberals in race relations discovered that they had no army with which to confront Powell's. They could muster a large number of letter writers to *The Times*, but no one, or nearly no one, to be counted against Powell in the opinion polls, still less in the streets. Labour Party officials whined in the Press about Powell's speech, but the Labour Party did not contemplate calling a demonstration to counter the pro-Powell demonstration of dockers.

Powell had conducted his argument, not in Parliament, but outside, to the public, in the country. The liberals fumed with rage about this boycott of Parliament. It was put around that Powell was 'afraid' to express his views about immigration in Parliament, where he would get 'torn to pieces'.

The truth more probably was that Powell regarded Parliament as irrelevant for his purposes. His appeal was addressed not to honourable members or to lobby correspondents but to the masses. One way not to reach the masses, Powell had learnt, was to speak in Parliament. While liberals complained of 'bad form', Powell, as countless demagogues had done before him, by-passed etiquette and Mr Speaker, and spoke straight to the masses.

There the liberals were powerless. All their strategy had been geared to work in private, to avoiding mass confrontation or public debate. When such a confrontation was forced upon them they could not fight back, and thus, after a frenzied and futile resistance in correspondence columns,' they joined the opportunists and has-beens in retreat.

Enoch Powell himself may well be defeated by his own pedantic foibles. But Powellism and worse to follow it has a good chance of victory as long as its opponents restrict the argument to the corridors of impotence. It can only be decisively and permanently defeated when its opponents seek to mobilize the masses, as Powell has done. Such a mobilization is quite possible. For the real reason for the widespread insecurity and distrust of politics, for the shortages which cramp the lives of all but a tiny minority, can be found – not in the immigration of black and brown workers but in the mean, ugly, elitist capitalism of which Enoch Powell as much as anyone is a champion.